AMERICA'S FAVORITE PAST TIME:
BASEBALL STORIES

AMERICA'S FAVORITE PAST TIME:
BASEBALL STORIES

DAN BARRUS

America's Favorite Past Time: Baseball Stories

Copyright © 2019 by Dan Barrus. All rights reserved.

No part of this publication may be reproduced, stored in a retrieval system or transmitted in any way by any means, electronic, mechanical, photocopy, recording or otherwise without the prior permission of the author except as provided by USA copyright law.

The opinions expressed by the author are not necessarily those of URLink Print and Media.

1603 Capitol Ave., Suite 310 Cheyenne, Wyoming USA 82001
1-888-980-6523 | admin@urlinkpublishing.com

URLink Print and Media is committed to excellence in the publishing industry.

Book design copyright © 2019 by URLink Print and Media. All rights reserved.

Published in the United States of America
ISBN 978-1-64367-839-9 (Paperback)
ISBN 978-1-64367-838-2 (Digital)

16.09.19

ADDITIONAL PUBLICATIONS
BY DAN BARRUS:

Everything I needed for Life, I Learned as a Scout

Wyoming's Best Kept Secret

Hunting and Fishing Bloopers

Memoirs of a Rescuer on the Second Rescue of the Willie and Martin Handcart Companies

Our Baker's Dozen (E-book only) *** *the story of the Tunney Barrus family*

Construction Hiccups—Part One (E-book only)

<u>Historical Novels :</u>   *The Willie Carson Saga*
  Jeremiah 2020, Big Sky Vigilante
  Gem State Warden, Paint Creek Prodigal
  Cloud Peak Refugees (due out in 2019)

CONTENTS

Preface 9
Chapter 1: What will I be when I grow up? 11
Chapter 2: Cody Enterprise at age 5 14
Chapter 3: King's Transfer and Storage......................19
Chapter 4: Cody Tire Co. 22
Chapter 5: Babe Ruth Ball 32
Chapter 6: American Legion Ball 43
Chapter 7: Headed to BYU to Try Out........................48
Chapter 8: Bogota, Colombia 51
Chapter 9: Husky Oil Company 56
Chapter 10: A BYU Walk-on 61
Chapter 11: Back to Husky Oil and Softball 66
Chapter 12: BYU and a Degree in Construction Management 69
Chapter 13: Graduation and Heart Mountain 72
Chapter 14: How about some Fast Pitch Softball?.....75
Chapter 15: Coaching My Children 81
Chapter 16: Little League and Politics.........................85
Epilogue 93

PREFACE

Shortly following the submission of my first four books for publication, I noticed that a big portion of my life was missing in those books. *Everything I Need for Life, I Learned as a Scout* was written about my Boy Scouting exploits. *Wyoming's Best Kept Secret* dealt more with my adventures while hunting and fishing in Northwest Wyoming. I followed those two books with a book titled *Hunting and Fishing Bloopers.* I still enjoy reading about the crazy things that happened to me while pursuing one of my passions. Hunting and fishing even though it has changed drastically was paramount in my life for many years. I also felt a need to share my feelings about the early pioneers that founded the Western United States in my book titled *Memoirs of a Rescuer on the Second Rescue of the Willie and Martin Handcart Companies.*

But I had not shared anything about another love I possessed while growing up. I lived and breathed baseball from the earliest days I can remember until the present decade. The sport has experienced many triumphs and major stumbling blocks over the years. But I still love to sit and watch a hard fought battle between a hitter and a pitcher. I can relate to each person on the field from the batboy to the head coach. I have experienced each position.

I want to dedicate this book to my Dad and all the Barrus ball players over the years. I have included some popular Yogism's (quotes from Yogi Berra) in each section which I relate to. I salute all those who have played baseball and softball, those who have coached, those who umpired, and to all the fans that have supported each of us over the years as we have participated in **America's Favorite Pastime.**

CHAPTER ONE

What will I be when I grow up?

I am sure that everybody has pondered that question at some point in his or her life. In my case, the deck was stacked from day one. I am convinced that I had a glove and baseball in the cradle with me when I left the hospital. My Dad's hero throughout his youth was Yogi Berra. Yogi was a MVP catcher that played for the New York Yankees. And that is what my Dad aspired to be. He was built very similar. Dad was short, muscular, and tough as nails; the perfect catcher. And just like Yogi Berra he could hit with the best of them.

My Dad was very talented as he progressed through school. He was the youngest boy in his family and learned how to catch by bouncing a baseball off the brick walls of his home in Winterset, Iowa. I visited that home early in my youth. I personally observed the broken pieces of mortar that had been dislodged along the side of the house facing their driveway. His brothers all had baseball fever at an early age. Baseball was the Barrus favorite pastime.

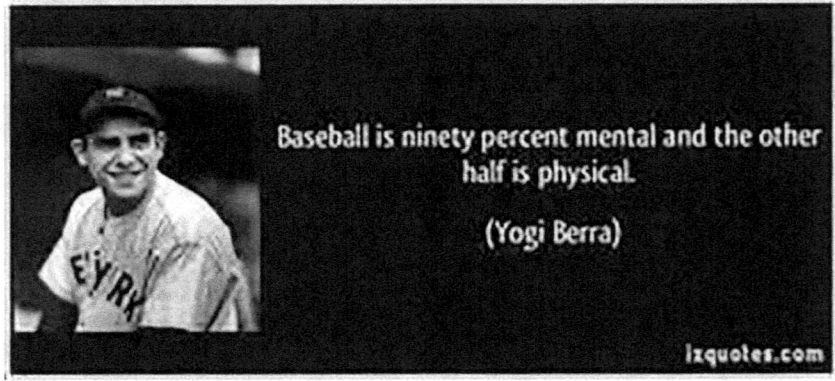

World War Two broke out when Dad was in High School. He found himself in the Philippines assigned to an artillery unit. While in the Army, he made a huge array of friends and built quite the reputation-playing ball. Upon his discharge, his brother Gabby talked him into coming to Wyoming. The hunting and fishing was the driving influence in moving to Cody. It so happened that the state of Wyoming had a baseball program that had multiple teams from different cities that got together and played each other. Of course, Dad was their permanent catcher. According to his fellow workers at the Husky Refinery, Dad had a designated parking stall just outside the left outfield fence. The story was that nobody parked their car there in order to avoid a broken windshield. Dad was a pull hitter and that was his power alley. So park there at your own risk. I can remember going to the ball field near the airport to watch his games. They all had uniforms, their own bats, and practice gear just like in the big leagues. But when they traveled to 'away games' they usually all jumped into a half dozen cars instead of a Greyhound bus.

As kids, we even got involved. During the games, the concession stand would pay 2-bits (25 cents) for any foul balls returned to them. Broken bats were of no use to the players so the local boys each tried to get their hands on as many as possible. A little tape rendered those bats as good as new to aspiring big league hitters like us. The envy of all the boys was their bat boy. He got to sit in the dugout with all the players and hear them talk baseball talk. Someday we each wanted to be that boy and feel important to the team.

My Uncle Gabby played on the team as well. His real name was Gene Albert Barrus. But with the first three initials of G.A.B. and the gift of gab, he always used his nickname wherever he went. Uncle Gabby was an avid photographer, sports announcer, and big game guide. He had photos as well as articles published in national magazines like 'Outdoor Life' and 'Sports Afield'. He called the play-by-play action of the high school sports teams for years. And his specialty when it came to guiding was the Pronghorn antelope. But to me, he was the star third baseman on my Dad's team.

Being related to two members of the baseball team gave me certain privileges not available to the other boys. One of those was to shag fly balls for the outfield as they warmed up. Gabby was really handy at hitting fly balls to just the right locations so the players could get their legs and arms ready to play. He would place the fly balls out in front of each fielder just far enough to make them stretch their abilities but not so far as to be un-catchable. After each outfielder took their turn, they would fire the ball back for Gabby to use again. He could easily keep 6 balls in play thus keeping the whole outfield busy. As the boy designated to shag the returning balls for Gabby, I was kept pretty busy myself. I would catch the returning balls then toss them back to Gabby.

I am really not sure how it happened or who was at fault. But on one of the cycles, I got too close to Gabby as he was swinging the baseball bat. He was driving the balls as far as he could so his swing was at full power. He didn't notice how close I was and POW! He caught me right on my left cheek! I went down like a ton of bricks! I really don't remember too much about the accident but Gabby thought he had killed me. There was blood everywhere. I do remember what I looked like for several weeks following the incident. I looked like I had a small baseball in my mouth. The side of my mouth was that swollen! But I recovered and continued shagging balls for the outfield whenever I got the chance.

CHAPTER TWO

Cody Enterprise at age 5

My Dad began his coaching career in the newly organized Babe Ruth League. He teamed up with a fellow refinery worker to coach boys from 13 to 15 years of age. The local newspaper, The Cody Enterprise, chose to sponsor them, which included a small fee to the league and equipment for the team. Those uniforms were quite simple by today's standards but each boy could hardly wait to put them on for the first game of the season. I can remember how pumped they all were because I was pumped sky high too. I had my own uniform as their bat boy.

I can remember what my responsibilities were. I needed to make sure all the bats were hanging from the bat rack inside the dugout. That is when they were not being used. I was to keep the dugout free of garbage and other trash, But most importantly I was assigned to pick up the bats of each player after they had hit. My assigned seat was just inside the dugout on the home plate side. Oh, I almost forgot another of my duties included non-stop chatter. I don't mean non-stop talking. By CHATTER, I was to shout encouragement to each of the players on our side of the field. In baseball circles there is a definite lingo that is used when the team is in the field as well as when we were up to bat. I needed to learn that lingo as quickly as possible.

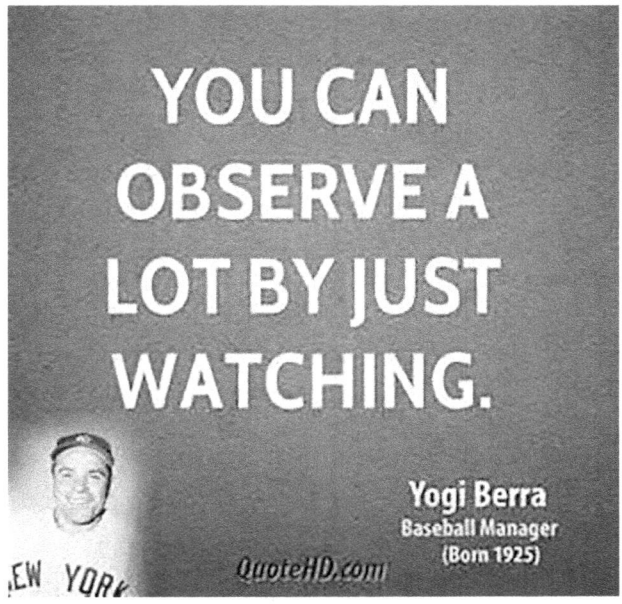

Our practices began in early spring. Many times the snow would make it difficult to see the ball. But the team kept on practicing in spite of the weather. I jumped right in, doing whatever they asked me to do. I would play catch with different players to warm them up. I must have chased a hundred foul balls during that first practice alone. It did take some time, but eventually I learned how to get all the gear into the equipment bag without any pieces being left out. And slowly but surely, I learned how to talk baseball.

I can still remember our first game against The Irma (a local restaurant that sponsored a team) I can picture in my mind's eye my uniform. It was gray with Blue lettering. The words BAT BOY were stenciled across my back shoulders with a large number ONE just below the title. I had a blue ball cap with a white "C" matching the rest of the players. The blue baseball socks were a little on the big side but I didn't really care. I had my first uniform!

We were the visiting team, which meant that we would be batting first. I had reviewed in my mind time after time, exactly what I needed to do after our first hit. I was perched on the edge of the dugout with every muscle in my body coiled for action.

Our first batter was walked on four straight pitches. Their pitcher was extremely nervous. His next pitch missed everything and their catcher had to chase it clear to the backstop. We had a runner in scoring position with nobody out. On the third pitch to Bill Blake he lined it over the second baseman's head. I bolted towards home plate concentrating on that bat lying there on the ground. As I picked up the bat to return to the dugout, I heard the Umpire yell, "TIME OUT!" It wasn't until then that I realized everybody was yelling at me instead of for the players. I was standing on the third base line right in the middle of the play at home plate! Everybody was trying to get me off the field so as not to interfere with the first run coming into score. The umpire called interference on me, not allowing the run to score and the runner was called out. I had blown my debut as abat boy! But I did learn a very important lesson. Wait until the play is over and THEN go get the bat!

My Dad was known around Cody as 'Tunney'. He picked up that nickname while he was still in High School back in Iowa. Dad was always trying to prove how tough he was. He ended up in quite a few fists fights. The Heavy Weight Champion of his day was Gene Tunney. They looked a lot like each other and the name stuck. Dad had a long scare down the middle of his tongue he received while fist fighting. He had a habit of clinching his tongue between his teeth. His opponent landed a swift upper cut that caught Dad's jawbone thus cutting his tongue wide open.

Tunney was well known in baseball circles throughout Wyoming. He spent 35 years coaching Little League Baseball and just as many years umpiring Legion Ball. He even umpired some while I pitched which must have been tough for him. But he was always fair, calling balls and strikes just as he saw them. I can remember pitching to Dad for hours on end. He had a nickname for me; as well, "Wild Man" My control over a baseball wasn't always my strong point. But I did manage to bring 'Heat' when I needed it. I spent just as many hours pitching to a worn out mattress as I did to my Dad or my brother, John.

Well anyway, back to my claim to fame as a five-year-old. That baseball season was totally captivating for me. The team continued to win and improve in abilities and camaraderie. I fortunately did not get caught making more blunders as their Bat Boy. Things were beginning to wind down for the team and the season.

I am not sure where the idea came from, but the players wanted to see how good I really was as a ball player. I had proven my abilities to them on the practice field. Now they wanted to insert me into their live game scenarios. But I was only five years old and they were all teen-agers! Somehow they talked the coaches into letting me play an inning on second base! And taking a turn at bat!

The novelty of it would wear off as soon as they saw a runt taking practice grounders at second base. But the opposing coach was fine with the change. It was probably because they were so many runs behind that there wasn't much of a chance that they would catch us. So there I was using my Dad's glove and hoping to high heaven that they didn't hit anything my way! I can remember thinking to myself, what will I do if the ball is hit to me?

The first batter wasn't a problem. Three pitches followed by three strikes. We had one out just like that. But the next guy up to bat posed another issue all together. He was much more aggressive at the plate. The first pitch was a high foul ball behind third base. That was followed by two consecutive balls. The count stood at two balls and one strike. Our pitcher decided to mix it up a bit. His next pitch was a change up. It completely fooled the hitter. He did manage to get a piece of the ball however. Guess where he hit it? That's right, it was a weak grounder and it was headed straight towards me at my position on second base!

It was like instinct or maybe lots of training, but I charged the ball as it slowly rolled my way. At just the right moment, I stooped and fielded the ball cleanly. I planted my right foot and threw a perfect strike to the first baseman. The runner was OUT by a mile. I can still get excited today about getting that out 50 years ago.

The last hitter popped out to the pitcher. Now it was our turn to hit. I was scheduled to bat third. Lee was up first, Bill was on deck, and I was in the hole! I can remember standing in the dugout, as my Dad reviewed what I had heard him tell dozens of batters before. But then he cautioned me about the possibility of a wild pitch. He didn't want me to get hit with a pitch and quite frankly I didn't want to get hit either. Lee ended up striking out on a full count. Bill flied out to center field, after three pitches.

I walked up to the plate with my helmet on and grit in my eye. I was scared too death but I couldn't let anybody see that. I had selected the smallest bat on the rack and choked up on the handle at least two inches. The bat was still too long for me but I didn't have any other choice. As I crouched over Home Plate, the strike zone became smaller than usual. The guy pitching definitely had trouble finding the strike zone. I walked on four pitches. Thank heaven!

As I headed down to first base, the coach reminded me not take too big a lead off the bag. There are two outs so I needed to be careful. I thought to myself. Careful of what? I stood on the bag and looked at the third base coach as he went through a series of signs. All I could think about was don't give me the STEAL sign! Luckily he didn't and I didn't have to show everybody how slow I really was at five years old. On the second pitch to my follow up hitter, he grounded out to the third baseman and the inning was over.

The ninth inning passed by without incident and the game was over. I had survived my first game without doing anything stupid! I was well coached!

CHAPTER THREE

King's Transfer and Storage

We had just moved to a new home on Shoshone Trail South. The neighborhood was filled with all kinds of kids our age. This was great because our house sat on a corner lot. The street converged around the corner making a perfect baseball diamond out of our side yard. And of course that is just what we used it for. The grass that had been planted there never stood a chance. Each base was ideally positioned and with constant use they were easy to pinpoint. The only limiting factor was the distance from Home Plate to the street. It was only 65 feet in dead away Center Field. But that didn't stop our games from involving everybody. All we had to do was to substitute a 'Whiffle ' ball in place of a hard ball. It took a well-timed swing and concentration to launch that hollow plastic ball into the street for a home run. Sandlot Ball was never as much fun as we had on Shoshone Trail South.

Everywhere we went we organized a baseball game. My grandparents had moved to Centerville by this time. So what did we do while the grown ups talked about the issues in the world? We played baseball. It didn't take much effort to find enough kids who wanted to play. And a neighbor's backyard provided just enough room to play Home Run Derby or even a game of Work Up. It was always a challenge to see how long I could stay up to bat while others were being put out left and right. The kids from Wyoming earned quite a reputation during that week in Utah.

Since I had turned six years old, I learned how to keep score. Not just runs, hits, and errors but the actual pitch-by-pitch account. Each week the Game of the Week was broadcast on Saturday afternoon TV. I would sit down with an old score book and record the play-by-play action from the television to a piece of paper. I thoroughly enjoyed watching those professional baseball games. It was probably due to the frequency of the teams chosen to air that I was converted to the Yankees way of doing things.

Yankee Infielders

My Dad's favorite player (Yogi Berra) was fun to watch. I remember great infielders like Bobby Richardson and Tony Kubek. Their defensive prowess was legendary. But watching hitters like Mickey Mantle, Roger Maris, and Moose Skowron; brought the game alive for me. By recording the actual pitch count from Whitey Ford and Sandy Koufax, I learned how to pitch to the better hitters. I observed how the best pitchers used their infielders to get those much needed outs instead of just trying to over-power each of them.

As a young pitcher on King's Transfer, I was called upon to throw strikes. Far too many of our games, ended up being a walk marathon. Those young hitters went up to the plate looking for a walk. I wasn't going to let that happen. By throwing strikes, I forced them to swing at my pitches. And because I was throwing fast balls most of the time, I had the ball past them before they had a chance to swing at it. I tinkered around with a curve ball and a change up, but my bread and butter pitch was a low fast ball. Many times I have been victorious because the hitters were scared to death I was going to hit them with my fast ball. And yes, I did hit several batters not on purpose but by accident. My Dad always insisted that I apologize to each and every one I pegged so as not to stir up anger or retaliations.

I also played shortstop when not pitching. My arm was good enough to throw out most runners on their way to first or trying to score after hitting the ball into the outfield. I was the cutoff man. The outfielders were to throw to either the shortstop or second baseman. They would either relay it to home plate to cut down the runner or catch it and then turn to gun down the hitter as he tried to stretch a single into a double. A lot of teamwork and communication was required. We all learned that each player had a place to be on every play. Whether it was assisting in the actual play or backing up the throws in case they were off target. We won more games using teamwork than by relying on the better players to carry the load.

I learned how to handle a bat better and better with each game played. Trying to hit the ball over the fence isn't the only way to win ball games. Many times just putting the ball in play will force the defense to make a play. Hits and errors are both equal ways to get runners on base. The batter just needs to get on base to keep their game alive! A walk or a single always results on a runner reaching first base and others runners advancing. The game of Baseball is simple and yet complex depending on the coaches and the players. But regardless, it is always fun to both play and watch.

CHAPTER FOUR

Cody Tire Co.

I began playing Little League Baseball at age 8. My Dad also began his Little League coaching tenure that same year. We carried the banner for Cody Tire Company. Their dominance began that year and ran for thirty-five years. Dad would end up coaching all eight of his boys while wearing the gray and red colors of Cody Tire. We began playing at the field on the east end of Stampede Avenue. Everyone knew about our sponsor, Cody Tire. Not because of our size, abilities, or dominance of the league. But because of our sponsor's sign in Center Field. It read," Cody Tire Co.—Hit over me $5." In all the years that I was in Cody, I only saw one home run hit over that sign. And I don't know if he ever received the coveted five dollar bill. That field has since been sold and the Little League Complex has been moved 'Below the Hill' next to the Legion Field and the Softball Complex. One of the Little League fields was dedicated to my Dad "Tunney" Barrus for his many years of coaching and umpiring baseball in Cody.

Little League Complex dedicated to "Tunney"

Just like in the Majors, a fierce rivalry can exist between two teams. The Yankees and the Dodgers or the Yankees and the Cardinals were some of the most intense World Series contests of all time. Even in their own division, the Yankees battled the Red Sox for a division pennant year after year. With famous pitching duels like Whitey Ford and Don Larsen vs Sandy Koufax and Don Drysdall. And the MVP many times was the pitcher that sealed the championship trophy like Bob Gibson over Mel Stottlemire.

When I began playing Little League ball, Cody Tire had Y Lumber as their archrival. And pitching face-offs between Meeker and Clayton or Barrus and Richardson, became the talk of the league. As an 8 year-old, I had to pay my dues just like any other drafted player. I have played my share of ball games out in center field or on short. I did get to pitch as a rookie, but I had to earn the right to go up against the bats of Y Lumber.

But a team that can't score runs doesn't win too many ball games. Cody Tire didn't have many power hitters. We learned in practice and game situations how to get runners on base. Once they were on, how to move the runners into scoring position. With a good bunting team, a single was as good as a double. And against a team with a weak catcher, many times a walk would yield a fast runner a trip to third. We also learned how to hit behind the runners. A runner on second could be moved to third simply by hitting the ball to the right side of the infield. Of course, if the defense wasn't paying close attention, that same runner would sprint into home and score another much needed run.

Cody Tire was known for strong defense. It would take a well-placed ground ball to get it through our infield. And our outfield was always helping each other out. Backing up every play on the bases was our strength. Each outfielder had a place to go no matter where the ball was hit or thrown. Many a runner was cut down by an outfielder catching a loose ball and firing it to the ever-ready infielders. They learned never to throw behind the runners. By throwing to first base instead of to third or home, would almost always allow another run to score.

As a pitcher, I had to work on throwing strikes. I had a strong arm and could throw my fastball past most hitters but if it wasn't in the strike zone it really didn't matter. I had to learn where each of the hitters that faced me couldn't handle my pitches. Low and on the outside corner was my favorite place to strikeout opponents. But coming high and inside can Handcuff a hitter with the same result. The thrill of getting three strikes past a hitter can be very satisfying especially if that player is one of their heavy hitters.

During the four years that I pitched in Little League, I relied mainly on my fastball. But I had begun experimenting with a curveball and a changeup as well. I was beginning to learn that a hitters timing is just as important to hitting as a good eye. As a pitcher, disrupting that timing can be crucial in getting that hitter out. A weak groundball is just as effective as another strikeout. A pitcher that can use his defense effectively usually wins more ball games than by trying to do it all by himself.

A No-hitter is a prize that all pitchers strive towards. I have thrown many one- hitters in my life, but I never did get a No-Hitter along side my name in the box score. I was able to face Y-Lumber twice during my last two years in Little League and come away with a one-hitter each time. The same opponent spoiled my bid for a No-hitter each time. Jim Fech! He was a good friend and a sound baseball player. And each time he spoiled my No-hitter it was on a sharp ground ball up the middle. He had learned that all he had to do was just meet the ball as it crossed the plate instead of trying to murder it. I can still see that grounder getting past our infielders and rolling into centerfield!

I spent most of my time studying Marv. He was their number four–clean-up hitter and the most dangerous hitter in the league. He had notched more home runs than anyone else. I just had to get him out, no matter what. I usually started him out with a fastball high and tight. That was usually good for a quick strike. Then I would try to get him to swing at an outside pitch. And then after I had two strikes on him, I would use my change up curveball to finish him off! He would always be way out in front of that pitch and end up pulling his head, badly. With his eyes off the ball, there wasn't any way he could hit that slow pitch. I must admit that I had his number every time he faced me. He was a good catcher and a player but I had been able to get into his head and come out victorious every time. I had several baseballs in my possession over the years that had the names and signatures of each player on my winning teams. I wonder where all those baseballs ended up?

At the end of my eleven-year-old and twelve-year-old years, we were both selected to play on the All Star Team. Marvin was one of the best catchers I would pitch to. He was well built and had quick feet and hands. He was a natural born leader. He was totally in charge of the entire defense from the outfield all the way to home plate. As an eleven-year-old, he would start as our catcher and hit again in the clean-up spot. I was used as a relief pitcher since we had an abundance of twelve- year-old starting pitchers. We had a lot of talent at every position.

The State Tournament that year was held in Cody. I was a little disappointed because I wanted to travel somewhere else in the state to play for the championship. But our team was the team to beat. It was a single game elimination—lose one game and you were out! I don't remember too much about that tournament except that we blew everybody out of the water. Cody had won its first Little League State Championship! I did get to pitch in a couple of the games but we were so far ahead of the other team it wasn't much of a contest. I do remember riding down Main Street in our new Fire Engine with the whole All-Star team loaded on top.

The next step following our state win was to the Regional Tournament in Boulder, Colorado. We would get to travel after all. It was 500 miles away and right next to Denver. We wanted to make Wyoming and Cody proud. No Wyoming team had ever won a single Regional Tournament game to date. To say we were excited is a gross under-statement. We all had new uniforms with matching windbreaker jackets. We crammed as much practice as we could into that next week. We were ready to play Boulder in Boulder.

Playing the hometown team on their own field combined with never having won at Regionals put us as a definite underdog. When we took the field that day in Colorado, we were just a little nervous to say the least. That first inning was scary. They scored four runs right off the bat. But our coach, Smoky Richardson pulled us all into the dugout to get us all settled down. Whatever he must have said, worked, because we proceeded to tie up the score at the end of regulation time. So into extra innings we would go.

According to Little League Tournament Rules, a pitcher can only pitch in so many innings per game That meant that each team would be using a different pitcher than the one they had been pitching with. Dewey Vanderhoff was moved to First base and Alan Richardson was given the ball at the start of extra innings. We hadn't been able to score in our half of the inning. Dewey was a hard throwing left-hander but Alan was a junk ball pitcher. He had several different pitches that he could deliver. And he would mix up the speeds as well which usually confused the hitters for a few innings. But the Boulder hitters adapted well. They were able to put runners on first and second with two outs.

After a brief time out, Smoky Richardson called out my name from the dugout. Alan had hurt his arm and I was sent to the mound. I was given as much time as I needed to warm up and then it was on with the game. My first pitch was a good foot over the head of the batter but Marv was able to catch it. He looked right into my eyes and gritting his teeth he just said, "Settle Down". I concentrated on his glove and then delivered a perfect Fast Ball right at the hitter's knees. With the count at one ball and one strike, I reared back a sent my next fastball towards the plate. The batter managed to make contact with the pitch and sent a one hopper to our centerfielder Ronny. He fielded it cleanly and then fired his own strike to Marvin, who was covering home plate. The runner was heading straight at him! He caught the ball with plenty of time to apply the tag but somehow in the ensuing play, the ball was knocked loose. The run counted and we had lost by one run in extra innings! What a heart breaker!

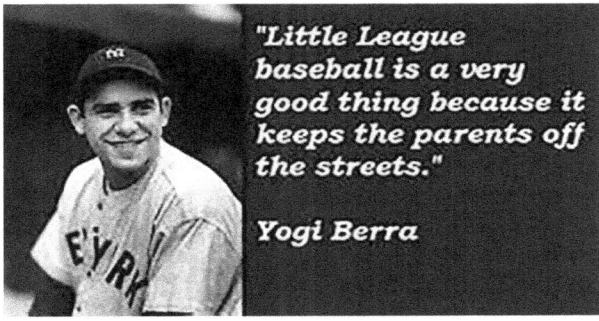

Parents & Baseball

As a twelve-year-old Little Leaguer, the summer took on a completely different tempo. I wasn't dreading the clashes with Y-Lumber but I was actually looking forward to each one. Cody Tire was sitting on top of the league mostly because of the team spirit that permeated the practices and each game we played. Nobody was playing for themselves alone but a team effort against each rival. Again I was on the mound each week against the best in the league. I was enjoying the season and looking forward to All Stars again.

We found out late in the season that the State Championship would be held in Laramie, home of the Wyoming Cowboys. Their baseball facilities were acclaimed all over the area. We had practiced hard and felt somewhat cocky as we drew Riverton for our first contest. They were always good but this year they had a real flamethrower scheduled to start against us. I was on the mound for Cody. I can still remember walking on the ball field and marveling at the beauty of the ballpark compared to what we were used to playing on. As we stood there, Marvin Nelson became mystified by how close the fences were. His enthusiasm to launch a few over the tall banner covered fences engulfed the entire team. Right then and there we should have recognized the writing on the wall.

As we drew the home team's dugout against Riverton, I sensed a feeling of momentum surrounding our pre-game warm up. I was ready to take the mound and show my stuff. I must have lost my concentration because on the very first pitch I got the ball up in the strike zone. It was promptly lined into left field and up against the fence. A stand up double to begin the game. It was like a bucket of cold water had been poured over my head. I was all business now! I promptly struck out the next two batters and got their clean up hitter to foul out to our first baseman. Boy, that was close. The first inning was over!

In our half of the inning, we showed our frustration. The first hitter opted out to the pitcher and he was followed by a weak dribbler to the second baseman. With two outs already I came up to bat. I swung at the first pitch and missed by a mile. I could hear my Dad holler," Stop swinging for the fence and just meet the ball." I never got a chance because I was walked on the next four pitches. But we had a runner on first and Marv was coming to the plate. Having a runner on just aggravated the situation. Marv struck out on the first three pitches he saw! The game was going to be a tight one!

The next three innings became a pitcher's duel. Both of us had zeroed in on the strike zone and set down each consecutive batter in order. But in the bottom of the fourth, we got a break. Our lead off hitter was hit by the first pitch he saw. We had a Runner on First with Nobody Down. The next batter turned the next pitch into a perfect sacrifice. He laid down a beautiful bunt to the first base side, which moved the runner up to second with just one out. Now all we needed was a single to take the lead. We didn't get the single we needed but their third baseman helped us out by launching a throw to first over the head of their player. An error allowed the first run of the game as well as our player to advance to third.

Our coach Smoky, called a time out. He had a substitution that he was sure would bring in that runner on third. Dick was well known for hitting long fly balls so he was inserted in to the line up for Davey. All Dick had to do was hit one of his trademark fly balls and the runner could tag up from third and score on the sacrifice fly. Dick watched the first two pitches go by but on the third fast ball he connected for a long fly to left. Their outfielder caught the fly just short of the fence and quickly fired it towards home plate. I can still see Smoky lining himself up with the base runner and their outfielder, and then just as the ball was caught he hollered; "Now" The Runner took off for home base easily beating the throw as it came in. The score now stood at 2-0 in our favor! I can remember thinking, that's just like they do it in the Pros!

As I took the mound at the top of the fifth, I can remember two relief pitchers heading down to the bull pen to begin loosening up in case I got into trouble. As if I was going to let that happen. I reached down for everything I could muster and began throwing BB's. Their hitters never stood a chance. With the help of a tight defense, I shut them down in order to preserve the Win! Cody 2 Riverton 0!

We had our first win of the tournament! Marvin and I had been assigned as roommates. Local families there housed each of the teams at the tournament in Laramie. Our host family just happened to live two blocks from the bowling alley. I guess you might guess where we spent our free time. The bowling was great fun but the pinball machines there caught Marvin's attention just as soon as we walked in the door. His Mom owned and managed a motel in Cody and Marv earned pretty good pocket change by helping out. I had spent the few dollars I had in my pocket but Marvin just kept on winning at this certain pinball machine. He had tunnel vision on using all the games he had won.

The following day we were scheduled to play Greybull. They were small in stature and nobody picked them to beat Cody. We were supposed to get picked up at eleven o'clock. But come eleven, guess where we were. We were still at the bowling alley playing that crazy pinball machine. Smoky finally found us and after collecting our gear we headed to the ball park. We were a good thirty minutes late! Marvin put on his catching gear and began warming up our starting pitcher, Davey. As I passed my Dad he grumbled," And where have YOU been?" I mumbled some lame excuse and took my position in the infield. I knew that conversation wasn't over by a long shot.

Again we were setting as the home team against Greybull. We took the field and completed the last of our warm up exercises. Davey was showing the same symptoms as I had during my first start as pitcher. He promptly walked the first two batters. Smoky made a trip to the mound in an attempt to settle his pitcher down. The third batter hit a ground ball to third base. Our fielder stepped on the bag and fired across to first but it was too slow. We did have one out however. Davey buckled down and struck out the next hitter. It was looking like we might get out of the inning unscathed when Davey sent his next pitch to the backstop. That wild pitch put two runners in scoring position with two outs. The infield was able to play at their regular depth since a force out to first would retire the side. On the fourth pitch, their batter hit a ground ball into the hole between shortstop and third Base. I quickly snagged the ball and rifled my throw to first base. But in so doing, I must have hurried my throw a little. It was too low to catch cleanly resulting in a throwing error to first base. They had scored a run on my error. With runners on the corners, they decided to try stealing second. Marvin was right on top of it and gunned him down without much effort at all.

The score stood at 1-0 throughout most of the game. They never did get another runner past second base. Each inning we sent hitters to the plate, we ended up leaving at least one runner in scoring position at the end of the inning. Our bats were quietly being silenced one swing at a time. When it came to the bottom of the sixth, we were down to our last chance. We managed to load the bases with only one out to go. Davey our pitcher came up with a chance to win the game for us. On his second pitch he connected on a screaming line drive to first base. Their first baseman stuck his glove up more out of defense than anything. Some how that ball stayed in the webbing of his glove. Nobody was more surprised than he was. The game was over! Greybull had somehow defeated the Tournament Favorite, Cody 1-0. They would advance into the championship game while Cody would head home from the single elimination tournament having been defeated. Cody had reached base safely with ten hits while Greybull had only managed two singles. Costly errors had cost us the ball game!

Greybull State Champs

CHAPTER FIVE

Babe Ruth Ball

Following Little League, Cody chose to join the Babe Ruth Organization. It is different from the Pony League that many of the communities in Wyoming used to transition their boys to the high school level. Boys from thirteen to fifteen years of age are allowed to play Babe Ruth ball. There are quite a few major differences between Little League and Babe Ruth baseball.

Probably the most noticeable is the size of the field they play on. The distance between the bases goes from sixty feet to that of ninety feet. The pitching distance is also increased from forty-six feet to sixty feet six inches. And the pitching mound is raised off the level of the rest of the field by a foot. Why the additional six inches is used, I haven't a clue. The fences are moved back distances from fifty to one hundred fifty feet. The game becomes much more spread out!

The players are permitted to wear steel cleats instead of rubber for better traction. And the runners are allowed to lead off the bases before the pitcher releases the ball! This creates a wide variety of teaching moments during practices and even more during those early games. Coaches spend hours teaching a runner when to lead off and how far. A constant game of 'Cat & Mouse' is ongoing as runners take their leads while the pitcher is attempting to throw them out before they can dive back in safely. There are a multitude of rules that must be followed by both the runners and the pitcher to make this incidental game of deception fair.

The length of the game is increased to seven innings. And just like in Cody, many of the games are played under the lights. This allows more people to attend the ballgames and more coaches to get involved since they don't need to take time off from work to coach. Babe Ruth ball resembles pro ball more than pony league ball, which develops a stronger, quicker player at an earlier age in my opinion.

Many of the communities that play Babe Ruth utilize 13-year-old tournaments that usually follow the regular season. Just like the name implies, the whole team is made up of thirteen-year-old players. These tournaments give the young 13-year- old boys more playing time thus helping them adapt to playing ball on a larger diamond. In my first year in Babe Ruth, I learned more than I thought was humanly possible. Pitchers are held to a very rigid set of rules that they did not bother with in Little League. The wind-up and pitching from the stretch had a very steep learning curve for me.

The wind-up I had been using in Little League was basically sound but I learned some refinements that really helped. Pitching is more about timing than I realized. The use of my entire body was needed in order to pinpoint my accuracy and increase the speed of my pitches. As I worked with various pitching coaches, I learned how to grip the ball differently depending on what I wanted the pitch to do. Mixing up speeds was a tool that I needed to master. I wasn't fast enough to just throw the ball by all the hitters. Deception had to be learned as I faced bigger and better hitters.

One tool that I implemented very early was how to use the pitching rubber for more leverage. Hooking my front cleat on the edge of the rubber and driving off that solid base improved both speed and accuracy. I also discovered the need to protect my cleats from the intense wear and tear of pitching. Repeated twisting, dragging, and planting of my right foot; was wearing my right cleat out prematurely. So a pitching toe was attached to my right cleat to help withstand the punishment used in pitching.

Right Pitching Toe on My Cleats

I learned how to use the mound to improve my accuracy as well. By watching where my left foot was planted on each delivery, I concentrated on repetition. If my left foot landed in the sane place with each delivery, my strike count increased. But if my left foot was landing all over the place, so were my pitches. I watched where my pitches were when they crossed the plate. If I was pitching repeatedly high, I would shorten up my stride. Conversely by lengthening my stride, I would consistently be able to deliver my pitches up in the strike zone. When my pitches were repeatedly outside the strike zone, I would start my wind-up farther to the right on the pitching rubber. And I learned to watch where my left foot was pointing as I released the ball. Just like sights on a rifle, if the sights aren't pointing at the target it is a pretty good bet that the target will not be hit. All these things go through your mind after each pitch. With constant practice, most of these tricks become second nature to good pitchers.

One of the changes in Babe Ruth ball is pitching from the stretch with runners on base. In the stretch, two motions are used with a definite rest in between each.

Pitchers need to learn the basics before they take the mound. I was certain I knew what to do from watching dozens of pitchers on the television. But sometimes watching and doing are two different things.

I can still remember the first time I had to pitch from the stretch in a game. I straddled the pitching rubber before beginning my pitching motion. As I began that motion, the umpire yelled," BALK!" That word is a red flag for all pitchers. It means they have broken a rule that all pitchers are required to follow. Each of the runners on base are then allowed to move up one base without being challenged. So now I had a runner in scoring position because of what I had done. Bill Blake, my pitching coach, called "Time Out" and came out with the umpire to explain what I had done wrong. The ump explained that I had to have my foot in contact with the pitching rubber during my delivery to home plate.

We all returned to our previous positions. I then placed my left foot on the pitching rubber. Again as I began my pitching motion, the umpire yelled," BALK!" Now what was I doing wrong? The umpire came out to the mound and explained that my right foot had to maintain contact with the rubber during my entire pitching motion. I finally understood but I now had a runner on third base instead of on first. I felt like I was knee high to a grasshopper. Everybody was laughing at me and pointing fingers. Embarrassing! I did finish the game and the inning with just one run scored against our team and me. I learned the hard way how to pitch from the stretch.

At least I thought I understood. The very next game that I pitched in would prove that I still had things to learn about pitching form the stretch. I had walked the first batter I faced. As I started my stretch, the runner on first just started running towards second. I turned to throw the ball to second base ahead of the runner. The umpire yelled, "BALK!" Oh No! I thought here we go again. My pitching coach came out to explain that I had to step off the pitching rubber backwards in order to do what I had just done. What else was I going to do wrong!

I didn't have to wait long. In the third Inning I walked another batter. As he was taking his lead off first base and with my foot on the rubber I faked a throw to first to get the runner to go back. You guessed it! The umpire yelled, "BALK!" Apparently while in contact with the pitching rubber a pitcher cannot fake a throw to an occupied base. My coach hollered from the dugout." Remember to step off the rubber backwards before you try anything fancy." So one by one I was learning the Do's and Don'ts of pitching, one balk at a time.

I developed the habit while pitching to always step off the back of the rubber to do anything except deliver a pitch to home plate. By so doing, it allows the pitcher to become just another infielder. I had learned that after making practically every mistake in the book. But I did not forget any of those lessons I had learned.

I played for Big Horn Paint & Glass while in the Babe Ruth League. Several of the friends that I played Little League with were on that same team. But then again several moved into the Legion program early. A boy plays better under some coaches' supervision than others. I enjoyed Bill Blake and Mike Fech as my Babe Ruth coaches. I also enjoyed playing with the Ballinger boys. Dave was my age and played in the infield with me. Garry and Larry were twins and played just about anywhere they were placed. Garry was a right-handed Utility Player while Larry was a southpaw. But they both hit from the right side of the plate. The Fech brothers, Joe and Jim also played for us. Joe was a year older than I was and did most of our catching, Jim usually played on second except when I was pitching then he was moved to shortstop.

Our roster consisted of small, fast, and aggressive boys; who all played the game well. We played SMALL BALL as it was called in the Majors. We didn't have anybody that could be classified as a power hitter. But we all knew how to get on base. A walk was as good as a hit. Then once there; we bunted, stole bases, and sacrificed in order to move runners up, eventually scoring. In so doing, we managed to down every team in the league. But our defense is what won most of our games. Strong pitching and teamwork was our trademark. We all played well together.

Just like in Little League, we had stiff competition. But Shoshone Title always seemed to present the biggest challenge. That was probably due to the Stahl Brothers. Curt and Rennie were a year apart in age but each pitched with equal results. They both had a rising fastball but Rennie had a killer curveball to go with his speed.

They had stumped our hitters time and time again. By the end of the season, we were usually dead even in the standings.

As a 14 year-old, I can remember looking up from that number two position at the end of the summer. We all committed to each other. Next year will be different, guaranteed! Our coaches both resolved to teach us how to hit Rennie's curveball. He had completely dominated us in that Championship game by allowing only two hits. Our offense needed to step up if we wanted to defeat them next year.

In our early season practices, Bill had each of our hitters move up in the box. His theory was to catch the curveball before it broke. He also had each of us choke-up on the bat. This would give us better control of our swing. His goal was to punch that curve through their infield. Mike went about the task from the defensive side of the team. He brought in a special pitching coach to work with just the pitchers. If Shoshone Title's pitchers could throw curveballs then so could we.

I was introduced to a completely different pitch. This Coach taught us to throw a curve-drop ball as we called it. But in the Majors, where he had played, it was just the standard curveball. He explained that by getting the ball to move vertically all we had to avoid was the three inches of bat thickness as compared to two feet of bat length with a flat curveball. We worked and worked at jerking this pitch with our wrist just like we were pulling down a window shade. He instructed us in the proper technique to be used when gripping the ball and our follow-through. The first game we used it in totally sent the rest of the league into a tizzy.

I can remember player after player wanting to know the secret behind our new drop-ball. Our Coach had warned us about giving away team secrets. It seemed like I couldn't get enough practice. I would take buckets of balls out to the homemade backstop we had made. A hundred pitches every other day was my goal. I had painted a strike zone on the mattress so I could keep track of the number of strikes I was throwing. I wish I could say that I never missed the whole mattress but that would be stretching the truth quite a bit. But I was continually improving week after week.

By the end of the season we were sitting with a comfortable lead over all the other teams in the league. We had to face Shoshone Title once again for the Championship. If we won, the tournament was over but if we lost we would have to play again. Our offense was able to take advantage of their errors and we built a three run advantage by the bottom of the seventh. All our defense had to do was finish them off 1-2-3 and the Game was ours. I had pitched the entire game up to that point. I picked a fine time to get wild. I proceeded to walk their number eight and nine hitters! Now I had to face the top of their order with a runner in scoring position!

Bill, our coach, called a time out. On his way to the mound he flagged off the infield and motioned for our catcher to stay where he was. He wanted to talk to me and me alone. His first concern was about my arm. I told him I felt just fine. He was looking at the ground in front of the rubber. He pointed out that I was under striding a little. He could tell by how my footprint was pointing towards third base. Point your foot directly towards the batter and things will be better, I promise!

After his visit to the mound, I took a big breath and took my sign. STRIKE! Shouted the umpire. I took my stretch and delivered. STRIKE TWO! was the call as the batter had taken a swing at my fastball. Everybody at the game was looking for my curveball. I shook off a couple of signs from my catcher. Then I delivered a perfect fastball high and tight. Another swing and a miss! I now had one out with Eric coming to bat. I hadn't been able to fool him at all with my pitches up to that point. He had already notched two hits off me and was coming up looking for another.

As I took my stretch, I was given the sign for a curveball. I hadn't started too many hitters off with a curveball. I shook off the sign. He countered with our sign for a fastball. Again I shook off the sign. I was confident that I really had Eric thinking now. What is he going to throw now? I took my stretch and looked in for the sign. There it was the same sign I had been given to start this hitter. I had set him up perfectly. I wanted to start him off with a curveball all along. I dropped a perfect curve on the outside corner of the plate. Eric was way out in front of the pitch. He hit a sharp grounder to third base. A perfect double play ball! Dave caught the ball with a single hop, a quick throw to second, and a snap throw to first. A perfect 6-4-3 double play! The game was over! We were the Babe Ruth Champions for good. As we all went around congratulating each other, it was just like it had been following all our other Games. We were a team and we had won as a team. Big Horn Paint and Glass—3, Shoshone Title—0

Babe Ruth All-Stars

That year as All-Stars we were headed to Casper. We had practiced hard and were ready to take on the State's Best fourteen and fifteen year olds. We drew our first game with the home standing Casper Team. We must have been too cocky because they blew us out of the water beating us by ten runs. After the game, we had a heart to heart chat with our coaches.

This was a double elimination tournament. A team had to be beat twice before they were sent home. By losing our first game, we had dug ourselves a huge hole to climb out of. As we looked at the losers bracket, we would need to play two games a day for the next four days to get into the Championship Game. Our coaches knew we were a better team than we had shown. The secret would be teamwork. We had all been playing by ourselves and not relying on each other. We all committed ourselves to the task.

We started out the next morning by downing a team from Greybull. Sound familiar? They called the game after five innings since we were almost twenty runs ahead. Then that afternoon we defeated another rival Powell. Those games were easy to get psyched for since they had been victorious against us in previous years. But our pitching was becoming scarce. Anybody that had pitched during the regular season was put into action. We continued on defeating team after team until we were scheduled to face Casper again.

They had been beat by a spunky team from Sheridan. We really wanted another shot at Casper following our first round drubbing at their hands. I had three innings of eligibility. I had faced these same hitters on day one and been shelled miserably. The coach decided that I would start again but I would be on a short leash. If I found myself in trouble for any reason, I would be pulled lickety split.

We were the visiting team, which gave us the opportunity to hit first. To my great surprise we hit for the cycle. All nine players reached base during that inning. The team had given me a nice lead, now all I had to do was hold it. My defense was eager and I had plenty to prove. We completely shut them down during my three innings. I am usually a strike-out pitcher but I had accepted the challenge from my coach to see how few pitches I could retire them on. I worked the entire three innings without walking anybody, not allowing any hits, and by throwing just fifteen pitches. Even I was amazed at our team. The coaches gathered us together following the win and told us that Casper was accusing us of playing a completely different roster from the one they had drubbed the first go around. We just laughed and prepared to face Sheridan.

Sheridan was well rested and threw their best at us. For four innings we kept it close, but eventually lost by three. We felt very satisfied in our performance and vowed to get revenge next year. Little did we know the rivalry that had been started that afternoon in Casper.

The following year in Babe Ruth was my last. I was playing on the same Big Horn Paint and Glass team with pretty much the same players I had the previous years. We picked up right where we had left off. We downed Shoshone Title in our first game and then proceeded to down team after team as we marched through the season. We found ourselves sitting in first place as the season was drawing to a close. We weren't cocky or anything close to that, we just knew we had the better team. A perfect season without a single defeat! A great way to end the league play!

We entered the District Tournament favored to take it. We did not disappoint. We ended up on opposite sides of the tournament bracket from Sheridan. There were not any teams that could play with us. We both downed team after team as we continued on a collision course with each other. The semi-final game matched Cody and Sheridan against each other. It was a close game with the lead changing hands several times before we reached the bottom of the seventh inning. Sheridan was the home team and we had used most of our pitching making sure to keep the game close. We had two outs and had their star hitter behind in the count. He managed to slice the next pitch towards right field. Our right fielder was fast and had a bead on the fly ball. But it was sinking faster than our fielder could adjust for. He dove for the ball but was inches short and the ball skipped past him as the runner headed for third. A stand up triple with their number four hitter coming to the plate!

I had been playing shortstop for most of the game but was inserted in as our pitcher, since I still had two innings of eligibility remaining. I had faced this guy several times before and had come off victorious most of the time. I quickly jumped ahead in the count. Now all I had to do was get him to swing at some pitches not quite in the strike zone. The next pitch completely fooled him but he was able to check his swing with the umpire agreeing with the first base umpire. I thought I had him! My next pitch was low and outside. a curve ball. The ball hit the ground just in front of our catcher and then jumped straight into the air.

Our catcher was up in a flash searching for the loose ball! He spun backwards looking behind the plate for the live ball. He still hadn't spotted it yet. It came to a rest about three feet off to the left of the plate. Marv started back to the backstop in desperation to secure the missed ball. Still searching for the ball he hadn't spotted yet. Everybody was yelling and pointing but still he didn't see the ball. The runner at third base hesitated and then broke for home. I saw what was happening but not soon enough. I headed towards the plate at a dead run in a foot race with the runner coming in from third. I reached the ball just as the runner took his last step towards the plate. Safe! Yelled the umpire. We had lost the game on a fluke missed ball that was laying three feet from home plate!

Our team was terribly disappointed but realized that we still had a chance. We were in a Double Elimination Tournament and only had one loss to our record. Tomorrow was another day. We showed up eager and hungry for revenge. We showed everybody there that we deserved to play in the Championship Game. We defeated them easily setting up the Grand Championship game the following day.

We were both ready to play and a real defensive struggle ensued. The score was tied 2-2 as we began the last inning. Again I found myself pitching and facing the heart of their batting order. The first player I faced was a piece of cake. Three pitches and three strikes... no problem! Their best hitter came up next. We had agreed before the game to only throw curve balls to him. But with the count at two balls and two strikes, he got a hold of my next pitch. It was a good curve ball but not good enough. He launched it into left field where it cleared the outfield fence by only a foot. We again had been beaten by just one run for the Championship. Sheridan 3 - Cody 2. Bummer!

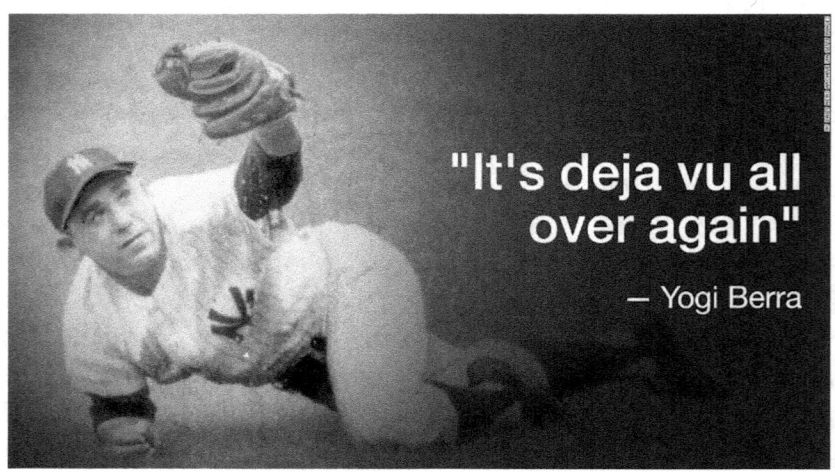

CHAPTER SIX

American Legion Ball

In Wyoming, High School Sports did not include baseball. Instead a summer league sponsored by the American Legion was in place. This gave us a chance to play ball for most of the summer months. We also kept our rivalries fresh. Our county rivalry with Powell wasn't much when it came to baseball. Cody ruled! But another team from Worland had some athletes and a competition was reborn.

They beat us soundly on the football field so we were out for revenge. The first time they came to Cody resulted in a blowout. Cody 15-Worland 5. I can still remember over hearing their star pitcher and coach. "The harder I throw the ball, the farther they hit it" We were primed for a clash in Worland.

We all loaded up in a dozen cars to make the hundred-mile trip to Worland. We fully expected a repeat of our lopsided victory. What ensued can only be described in one word…UGLY!!! We did not play well at all! We were arguing with each other and blaming the umpires for every bad call that was made. We ended up losing by one run in extra innings. But the worst part was how we handled defeat. The majority of the players vented their frustration by joining in a brawl near the pitcher's mound! Even the coach got mixed up in the whole mess! Threats were made from both sides and the police had to separate the teams. And this is high school ball.

The second game of our double header was postponed a day. And we were escorted out of town by a couple of police cruisers! The parent's committee called an emergency meeting with the intent of firing the coach and canceling any future games between the two teams. Cooler heads prevailed however. A chartered bus was hired to transport the entire team and coaches back to Worland the following day.

Before we left the bus that day, our coach apologized for his temper and the fiasco of the previous day. His final words to us were totally graphic. "Now we are going to go kick their butts, then load up and return home P D Q."

Since we were the visiting team, we would be hitting first. We should have known what was in store for the first pitch...a bean ball aimed right for the helmet of our first batter! The umpire stopped the game immediately and issued a warning to both teams concerning the type of baseball that would not be tolerated. Then we proceeded to dominate the game. The game was called after 5 innings with Cody ahead by fifteen plus runs. We all loaded up in the bus and headed straight home! A packaged lunch had been prepared so we didn't even have to eat in town or nothing. The rivalry was over for that year.

But the following year found us at it again. Both teams were battling to determine superiority. Pre-season, mid-season, and finals; we always seemed to see each other at least once and the outcome was usually just a run apart. The series I remember the most was on a neutral field. Both teams found themselves in strategy right down to the last out. I had pitched my allotment of innings and I was grateful for the rest. My shoulder and right arm were spent. I probably hadn't conserved my rest between games properly. I noticed my muscles were stiff and taking forever to get loose. But when our new coach asked me if I had anything left, I acknowledged that I might have a little left in the tank. But deep down I dreaded the possibility. He explained that I would not be able to pitch unless the game went into extra innings. I didn't understand but prepared for the inevitable.

Sure enough, at the end of the nine innings we were locked in dead even in runs scored. In the top of our half of the inning we managed to squeeze a single run across. Our defense managed to get two outs but in so doing had loaded the bases. I had been sent to the bull pen to get ready. It was taking forever and I wasn't sure I should go in. But when the coach sent for me I responded. The pitcher that had started the inning had developed a huge blister on his throwing hand. I entered with the count even at two balls and two strikes. I didn't want the count to go full so I discussed my options with my catcher. He knew the batter well. He loved fastballs out over the plate. We agreed to oblige.

My best fastball against his over-confidence to win the game. I can remember concentrating on the glove that was calling for the pitch, letter high and tight inside. As I delivered the pitch I felt that stiffness hindering my motion. The pitch had every ounce of mustard I could give it. It entered the strike zone and began tailing to my right. The movement on the ball was just what I needed. The batter stepped into the pitch but his bat was moving too slow. Strike Three! I had saved the game with just one pitch! We had sent Worland down for the last time that year!

The traditional rivalry between Cody and Powell surfaced again the following year. It was probably due to Cody's football team getting demolished at Cody. The basketball team did fair much better. The baseball program was where Cody continued to dominate. We had owned the baseball diamonds for several years. Powell had a mental block when it came to baseball. Cody always won and that's just the way it was.

I can remember one of the last games of my High School days. Powell was scheduled to play us in Cody at the legion field below the hill. It was a night game and Powell supposedly had a new ace on the mound that we had never seen before. He had played in Utah and Montana both. We didn't know what to expect. That is until the bottom of the first inning. His control was pretty good and he had a moderate to good fastball. But his curve ball was lights out. Both teams managed to stay even through eight innings.

I was handed the ball at the beginning of the eighth inning and their new ace was moved to third base. It was my job to shut their bats down like I had done time and time again. One of their better pitchers entered the game and the pitching duel was on. We each pitched well with no runs being scored for the following four innings. Then I was scheduled to hit first in our half of the inning.

Every once in awhile a ball is hit to just the right place on the field that nobody could quite get to it. It doesn't have a lot of speed as it leaves the bat. It just seems to have eyes of it's own. That is what happened to me. I managed to put some wood on the ball and it did the rest. I ended up on first base without even a throw to get me out. The next couple of pitches were called strikes. Then the ball was grounded to the second baseman. He fielded it cleanly but due to the slow nature of the ground ball he chose to make the play at first. I was on second now with just one out.

Our next hitter had been on fire for several days. It seemed like everything he hit found it way into a hole somewhere. The whole team was poised for a game winning single and the game would be over. But the cards were stacked against him. He took a couple of pitches for strikes. He argued about the call but the count stood at one ball and two strikes. The next pitch was in the dirt and their catcher made a beautiful stop to keep the ball from going clear to the backstop. I was signaled to move up to third base on the error. The field was set and the next pitch was fouled to the third baseman. Now we had two outs. But we still had a runner in scoring position.

Our next batter had pretty good speed and had beat out many a slow groundball. All we needed was one run! Their infield was moved back to normal playing depth since they had two outs and a ground ball would be an easy out at first. They were in good position to send the game into the twelfth inning. But the game sometimes is decided in the most unusual ways. Their pitcher had a pretty good curve ball and he was using it a lot. Maybe too much.

His next curve bounced in front of the plate and headed straight up into the air. It must have hit the front edge of the plate or something. I wasn't sent home by the third base coach or nothing. I just took off on my own. The catcher had a bead on the ball but there must have been some spin on the ball or something because he failed to field it cleanly. He finally grabbed the ball when we were both about equal distance from the plate. The play was going to be close. I dove head first while reaching for the corner of the plate. All I heard was the umpire as he yelled," Safe", while spreading out his arms!

We had won another game against Powell in a completely different manner than most.

As the team rushed out to congratulate me, I was wiping my face and mouth to get the dirt out of my face. I was spitting dirt and coughing a little. I must have forgotten to close my mouth as I dove into home! I was a sight! But hey, we had won!

CHAPTER SEVEN

Headed to BYU to Try Out

"When you come to a fork in the road....take it"
—*Yogi Berra*

I had spent the last half of my senior year sending out letters to several baseball programs around the area. I was hoping for a scholarship to play baseball and while there I hoped to pick up a degree in something I was interested in. I hadn't heard from any of the schools except BYU. Coach Tuckett replied that he had distributed all his scholarships but he would still like to see me when I arrived in Provo.

I could tell he was a little disappointed in my height. I am only 5 foot 7 inches if I stretch as tall as I can. Most pitchers in college and the majors are somewhere between 6 foot and 6 foot 6 inches. Being tall makes it much easier to develop the timing needed for control and to utilize leverage, which results in better ball movement. But I was at least given a chance to prove myself.

I enrolled in several classes keeping my afternoons open so I could practice with the rest of the recruits and hopefully make the team. There must have been thirty or forty guys there from all over the United States. And you guessed it; I was the only one there from Wyoming. I overheard a couple of the asst. coaches talking one day. They just didn't think I could compete since baseball was only played for three months each year in Wyoming. But they didn't know how committed I was.

Week after week passed with dozens of players being released from the try-outs. But I continued to work hard and concentrate on the basics of good baseball I had learned over the years. It was turning colder now that the month of October was over. The rest of the pitchers were complaining about the cold. Hey, this is what it is like in Wyoming all the time. I was showing what I could do. I had made it through several cuts as the ranks of recruits were whittled down to the final few.

There was to be one more cut before the Thanksgiving break. The freshmen pitchers were going to pitch in a simulated game against last years starting nine. Now these guys knew how to hit. I had faced several of them already over the course of the fall workouts and had managed to give them all they could handle. I was ready for battle!

As I was warming up, I felt strong and ready for the challenge. But as I began to pitch to the lead off man, I couldn't throw a strike for the life of me! I walked the first three hitters! This was turning out to be a real nightmare. I noticed the head coach chatting with the next hitter. I was sure he was telling him to take the first strike. I made adjustment after adjustment to guide my pitches across the plate. Nothing seemed to work. I was finally pulled after I had walked seven straight batters. I was completely devastated. I was beating myself up for the next hour of practice. I had been terrible and I knew it. At the end of practice, I was notified that the coach wanted to see me in his office. I knew what was coming. I entered the coach's office and listened as he explained his baseball program to me. And then I heard those words that I knew were coming. "I hate to do this, but you are not quite ready to play ball for BYU, we need to cut you from the team!'

I was shell-shocked. I hadn't been cut from any team before. I knew I was good enough to pitch at BYU but for some reason I had lost my control and that is the most important tool that a pitcher thrives on. I had a tough time concentrating on my classes and felt some relief when Thanksgiving began. I headed home to talk over the whole experience with my Dad. He was disappointed to say the least and encouraged me to give it another try next year. That was not meant to be however. At the conclusion of my five-day vacation, I received a telephone call from Bishop Fillerup. He wanted to see me before I returned to school.

As we talked, I felt totally relaxed and calm. That is unusual for me when talking with my bishop. He had something on his mind and he knew that I knew it. I didn't have to wait long. "Dan, I want to call you on a mission for the next two years!" I looked him straight in the eye and replied that my schedule had just been freed up and I would in fact serve a mission for the Lord!

On my way back home to tell my parents, it hit me right smack in the face. That's why you couldn't throw a strike that last day of practice. The Lord wants you to be a missionary!

CHAPTER EIGHT

Bogota , Colombia

*"Why buy good luggage, you only
use it when you travel"*

Yogi Berra

My mission call was to Colombia/Venezuela, and I entered the Mission Home in January of 1971. My first two months would be learning Spanish in the LTM back in Provo, Utah. I spent every waking moment trying to think in Spanish. I finally achieved that but it didn't happen as quickly as I had hoped for. I can remember dreaming in Spanish about 3 months after I arrived in South America. I had heard of missionaries that dreamt in Spanish and never thought I would perform that coveted action. But I did and it was really quite plain and ordinary. The setting for my dream was in South America and everybody around me was speaking perfect Spanish and that included yours truly as well.

I can remember leaving for the Mission Field with a real sense of confidence. I had learned more about the gospel than I thought was possible and I felt completely at ease speaking Spanish to those around me. I was to get a real eye-opening experience in the airport in Miami, Florida. I boarded the airport next to a couple of Puerto Ricans that were speaking Spanish. They were talking so fast that I could hardly hear a break in between words. My confidence level took a real nosedive. In less than an hour, I had to go through a customs check in Caracas, Venezuela. Everything would be in Spanish and I was supposed to be fluent. HELP!

I did get through the airport without any really embarrassing things happening to me. And the next day I was out on the streets of Caracas talking with the locals. I really didn't talk that much and I had a real tough time understanding them. But, Hey, I was on my mission. I remember meeting with my Mission President to get acquainted. I expressed a deep desire to serve somewhere cheap! At that time the costs for every mission was set by the individual mission and not equaled out church-wide. I breathed a huge sigh of relief when I was informed that my first assignment would be in Bogota, Colombia!

My second day in South America was spent flying from Caracas to Bogota. Bogota is the capital of Colombia and has a population approaching ten million people. That is a huge step for a kid from Wyoming and a town of less than ten thousand. My first area was in Ciudad Kennedy. I thought it strange to name a suburb of Bogota after an American president but that is where I would spend the next four months. There were dozens of blessings from that assignment. The cost was less than a hundred dollars a month, the people in Bogota speak much slower than other countries, and Ciudad Kennedy is situated on the outskirts of the city. The only time I would be downtown was occasionally on our preparation day. I almost forgot to mention the food. No tacos, no burritos, no spicy hot food at all. The basic diet in Colombia is rice and soup. And dinners consisted of chicken and rice with beef every once in a while. They did eat a wide variety of fruit some of which I enjoyed and others I never did acquire a taste for.

I was transferred to Medellin for my second assignment. I had to learn Spanish all over again. These people had an accent that was difficult to pick up. I must have accomplished it because all the way through my mission I was identified as being from Medellin because of the accent I developed. And no there was not a drug problem there then like exists today. It was still a large city of 6 million and I was placed in the heart of the city.

One of the smallest areas in the mission was on the East side of Medellin. The missionaries there were always looking for new people to teach. They had tracted along every street two or three times. One of the missionaries in the area came up with a novel way to meet people. He organized a junior baseball league for youth 12 years of age and younger. (Sounds a lot like Little League) He had funded the league through donations from Utah. We had a blast teaching them baseball and getting to meet their parents. Our games were held on Saturdays.

I can remember how eager they were to learn this new game. During one of our first games, the crowd got involved a little too much. One of the batters hit a foul ball near the foul line along first base. The young players were each trying to catch the foul ball when a spectator entered the playing field and attempted to catch the ball with his bare hands. In so doing, he knocked one of the young players to the ground. I became quite agitated over the whole situation and inserted myself into the malay. The spectator refused to leave the playing field insisting that he was going to take the ball home with him. The spectator wouldn't leave until I gave him a solid push backwards explaining again that the game was for the youth to play and not the adults. He returned to the safety of the crowd while yelling. "Look, everybody! This is how the Americans help us out. By playing with children" At this point a large group of the spectators turned against the lone agitator and proceeded to put him in his place. They truly appreciated what we as Americans were doing with these boys!

From Medellin I was sent to Cucuta. It sits on the border between Venezuela and Colombia. It is probably the smallest city in the mission. It was the site of the 1972 Pan American Games. They are very similar to the Olympics but scaled down in size. The only countries involved are in Central and South America. They had built stadiums and fields totally state of the art to hold all the spectators and participants. At that time, the use of the facilities was on a reservation basis only. As missionaries we reserved the gyms and fields at every opportunity.

I was sent to Cali from Cucuta. It is located near the border with Ecuador. I served in two different areas while in Cali. One of those was along side a Colombian Air Force Base that housed hundreds of pilots, mechanics, and maintenance personnel for the government forces stationed there. My companion and I were sent to the area at the same time with the previous missionaries being assigned to different areas. We had to start from scratch.

We were quite a distance from the center of Cali and did not enjoy the 45-minute bus ride into the city to play basketball or soccer with the other missionaries. So after some discussion, we decided to purchase two baseball gloves and begin playing catch every morning before we began proselyting. This was a great change of pace for each of us and very enjoyable. On one of those early morning activities, a local fellow stopped to watch us for a few minutes. At the conclusion to our exercise, he invited us to come play baseball with his team over at the Air Force Base. This would prove to be much more than we had anticipated.

At first, we just joined them for some batting and fielding practice. But they could see that each one of us had played the game before. Practice games were organized and one thing lead to another. Pretty soon we were given uniforms and invited to play with them in an organized league. We were developing quite a relationship with several of the players. One of those was their catcher. He asked me on one Saturday afternoon if I had ever pitched. I was soon inserted into their starting rotation and developed a reputation as a Gringo Pitcher. My fastball was better than anybody in the league and my curveball was unhittable. At least that is what the newspapers were saying.

When I was not pitching, I was playing third base. My batting average was hovering between .330 and .340 and I was hitting directly behind my companion. He was a better hitter than I was. He had hit several round trippers while I had only managed to hit the fence once. But we were staying in shape and teaching several of the players the gospel lessons. They had arranged to let us copy pamphlets and flyers for the mission home by the hundreds. And they always wanted us to come eat at their cafeteria. They claimed that the food was American. (we didn't have the heart to tell them that the food was just average and definitely not American) They enjoyed having us around and we enjoyed being around them.

We had been together as companions for close to four months. A change was due any time now. The baseball team was scheduled to begin its final tournament of the season. We were sitting in first place and the whole team claimed that it was because of 'Los Gringos" but we knew that a team needs more than two good players to win a tournament. We always kept an eye on the local newspaper in order to keep track of our competition. The latest headline was about the Gringo pitcher from the state of Wyoming that had pitched twenty-nine innings of shutout baseball. The caliber of the players in the league wasn't as high as most college players but twenty-nine innings is still twenty-nine innings.

We received word that a Major League scout from Montreal wanted to talk to me after our next game. Imagine that, coming all the way to Colombia to talk to a scout from Canada. Stranger things have happened. Sure enough after our next game, I ended up talking about future baseball plans with this professional scout. Maybe after my mission, anything could happen.

Our championship game was scheduled to be played on a Sunday. The whole team knew that we didn't play on Sundays. They were convinced that if we didn't play they would get beat. We knew different than that. They played the game and came back triumphant! Champions! I even took a picture of the trophy as proof. But the greatest success was how widely we became known. We had a hard time getting into homes to teach before our playing on the team. Now we had a hard time fitting all the discussions into a weekly planner. We were the top baptizing companionship in the mission and attendance at Sacrament Meetings had doubled since we had arrived into the area. It was a grand time but we were split up shortly there after.

I was sent back to Bogota to finish my mission. The baseball programs became a thing of the past and I never did hear from that Montreal Scout again. Back to Wyoming I went. I had laid a strong foundation for future service in the church and my mission was a success.

CHAPTER NINE

Husky Oil Company

"The Future Ain't What It Used to Be"

Yogi Berra

Upon returning to Wyoming, I found things had changed. Well, I had changed but the people there expected me to be just the same as I had been before my mission. A big adjustment was needed by everybody involved. I wanted to see the ward I had grown up in, change and be more missionary minded. I was totally taken back by how much my parents had grown older. Two of my siblings had been born while I was in Colombia. I expected all my friends to be there. They weren't in Cody anymore. They were serving missions and working on college degrees. I had to adjust to a new way of life.

I felt the need to finish my studies at BYU. I didn't have the monies needed to get back in to school. Dad helped out by having a temporary job waiting for me when I walked off the airplane. He was quite proud in his own way of the things I had accomplished. He really wanted one of his boys to follow his footsteps working at the refinery. Husky Oil Company had been good to our family. Dad fully expected the refinery to be in Cody forever. I could see the end coming and it was closer than we all expected.

My first day of work at the refinery was a classic 'Show and Tell' episode. Stan, my boss, spent most of the morning parading me around to multiple stations showing me how it all fit together. He made it a very significant point of highlighting the areas of the refinery that my Dad was over. There was some definite competition involved. I would work under Stan for the better part of that summer until I landed a promotion to the 'Rack'. I was still loading asphalt for shipment around the United States but the 'Rack' was were the tanker cars were loaded. It involved shift work and there was a small pay raise too. I was to spend the next three summers working at the Husky Refinery to help pay for school.

But the strangest part of working at the Husky Refinery was the chance to organize a softball team from the employees of the refinery. That first summer was definitely different. The softball league was playing on a field that had 'Short' fences. If a regulation softball had been used, every other pitch would have been hit 'over the fence'. Somewhere they came up with the idea to use a larger ball. A ball with a circumference of sixteen inches was used. It became practically impossible to hit that ball over the fence. The ball was so large that when a batter hit it, the ball would begin spinning and take on an elongated shape. The centrifugal force was so pronounced that as soon as it would touch a glove it would ricochet out allowing the runner to advance on the 'Error'. Different types of gloves were used to help control the violent spinning of the ball but usually to no avail. I even saw fielders attempt to smother the ball with their bodies. It really took a lot of concentration to catch that spinning gyroscope while on defense.

The play I remember the most was a total gymnastic routine by itself. My friend, Bill was playing for Husky and had helped organize the team. He was a large man tipping the scales at well over three hundred pounds. The play I remember happened on a rainy night with the lights on. Bill was playing center field that night. We had two outs when their top slugger came to bat. The entire outfield backed up anticipating a long fly ball. After a couple of pitches, the hitter sent a 'spinner' into short centerfield. Bill came running in to make the catch. Suddenly, he realized that he had misjudged the flight of the ball. He could see that the ball was hit harder than he thought and was heading over his head. He attempted to put on the brakes.

As he planted his feet to stop, they both began to slide on the very wet grass of the outfield. Bill was sliding first on his left foot and then on his right. During all of the sliding, his arms were flailing like a windmill in a hurricane. This scene ended abruptly when Bill reached out and grabbed the ball in full flight. He had the ball in his glove hand but the wetness of the grass then totally gave way and his feet shot out from under him. All three hundred fifty lbs. of Bill were lifted up in the air at least four feet and then just as quickly, it all came down with a totally prone belly flop and a huge splash.

I was playing shortstop at the time and was running out to help with the play. I saw the entire scene unfold as I explained. But what happened next was the clincher. Bill had control of the ball all the way until he hit the sod. I saw the ball trickle out of his grasp a couple of feet. But just as fast, I saw his right hand shoot out and grab that ball. Everybody was running to help Bill having seen the collision he had with the soggy field. They were certain that Bill had hurt himself drastically. The umpire came running up behind the play signaling that the 'Catch' had been made. I must have been the only one on the field that saw what really happened. But who was I to take away Bill's miraculous catch that ended up winning the game.

Even though this softball league had different rules, it provided an outlet for family summer activities. What would evolve was something Cody needed. But that first summer, it was all about competition. A lot of the players that I had played with over the years, decided they would group together a team of the better baseball players and dominate the new league. Jack's Sports was the team to beat. As an organizer of the Husky Oil team, I devoted many an hour in strategies about that very objective. I feel like the Husky team was similar to the Bad News Bears of Cody Softball.

Most of our players came from the working class. They played to have fun and if they won it was just icing on the cake. But I had been brought up to win. So I implemented a few wrinkles to help give us an edge. The game was slow pitch softball. The pitcher was required to put a high arch on each pitch. I felt like this caused each batter to PULL his hits to the left side of the diamond. I decided to employ a SHIFT with our defense to take advantage of this left field tendency. We pulled our right fielder into center field with the other outfielders all shifting to the left side. We left our first baseman fairly close to the bag so he could quickly move to the bag and receive the throws from the infielders on ground balls.

Our pitcher was as much a part of the defense as any of the players. He concentrated on placing his pitches on the left side of the plate thus aiding our defensive alignment. And as soon as he released his pitch, he would move to his left. He would help field where the second baseman usually played. It worked really well for the first half of the season. The batters were frustrated by the SHIFT and became easy outs. But Jack's Sports adapted quickly.

They spent hours practicing their inside out swing. They could see the defenseless right field open and knew they could take advantage. It took them about three head-to-head match ups before they were beating us at our own game. So we switched to a random shift defense. We would only shift for certain hitters or on certain situations. I even implemented a signal to the defense for the shift to be implemented. It became quite the game of Cat and Mouse. But it was all in the name of FUN.

The climax of that softball season came with a final championship game against Jack's Sports. We each knew the strengths and weaknesses of each other. Putting all the trickery aside, it boiled down to which team could execute the basics the best. That is why the outcome was so unpredictable.

In baseball and most softball games, there is a rule called the infield fly rule. With runners on first and second, or first, second, and third; any pop fly to the infield is ruled an automatic out. For whatever reason, the league decided to set this rule aside. It would be this decision that would cost us the game. Let me describe the situation.

The score was tied and we were at bat in the bottom of the sixth inning. If we scored, then we would win. We were determined to prevail and promptly loaded the bases with nobody out. A hit or even a sacrifice fly would bring in the winning run. We had one of our best long ball hitters coming to bat. On the first pitch he was given, he really stepped into it. But he must have dropped his back shoulder or something. The ball was popped up to the third baseman. (Remember the infield fly rule was NOT in effect) The third baseman knew this as well. It was an easy out. But the pop fly was dropped intentionally! This forced all the base runners to try and advance to the next base. But in the confusion that was generated, each of the three base runners were tagged out before they realized what was happening! A Triple Play! The ball game forced into extra innings and we came up short. Jack's Sports had out foxed us in the end!

CHAPTER TEN

A BYU Walk-on

*You don't have to swing hard to hit a
Home Run. If you got timing, it"ll go.*

Yogi Berra

Following that summer of work and softball, I hired out as a professional big game guide. I went on three hunts into the Thorofare Country. And another three hunts out of the Castle Rock Ranch. I enjoyed the experience while learning more about myself and the high country near Yellowstone Park. But I still had a desire to prove I could pitch baseball on a higher level.

I returned to BYU and promptly paid a visit to Coach Tucker to talk baseball. He remembered me from before my mission. He made no promises but agreed to let me show up for a chance to play. I also met with Coach Plunkett who was coaching the JV squad. All went well and I was able to get my foot in the door.

I showed up at the Smith Fieldhouse expecting to begin working with the team. Instead I was introduced to Nate who was also a walk-on. An assistant coach reviewed with us the schedule that we would be following. To loosen up, we needed to jog two miles at half speed around the indoor track. Following that we would run the straight-aways of the track at full speed and walk the curves. Another two miles was knocked off this way. We then grabbed our gloves for a half hour of 'Soft Toss' with each other. Finally we were directed to jog another two miles again at half speed and that was practice. We were a little taken back by the low intensity of the work out but we continued to follow this routine for the first two weeks.

We finally met the catchers of the team during the third week of practice. We were shown the indoor pitching mounds and spent that next week throwing at ¾ speed with nothing but straight stuff to our catchers. Of course we began and ended our practice sessions with a two-mile run. A pitcher needs to keep his legs in shape so as not to put too much strain on their arms.

During the month of February, we were allowed to show our catchers what we had. Finally getting to pitch at full speed! We didn't get to face any batters yet but spent that entire month pitching. We were encouraged to work on new pitches both from the stretch and our full wind-up. The catchers were keeping track of our balls and strikes, without each of the pitchers knowing about it. About half way through February, we were introduced to several other Pitchers. I would get to know Jack Morris and Veldon Law well during the course of the next few months. Several pitchers came and went but these guys were to make up the starting rotation for the JV Team along with Nate and myself. At the end of February, we were handed a blue ball cap with a white "Y" on it. We had made the team!

We moved outside in March and began working out with the entire team. Practicing defensive drills and throwing to live hitters. Oh, I almost forgot the two- mile runs every day; a guy has got to stay in shape. The infielders and outfielders were working on different drills while the pitchers ran. We held a few practice games over the next couple of weeks. The pitching rotation each took their turn pitching to rest of the team. I learned quickly that Vance Law, Lee Org, and Doug Howard were our toughest outs. They could hit.

We started our league play by inviting Orem Technical College to Provo for a double header. Each of our starting pitchers was given three innings to begin the season. I was very nervous and afraid that I might lose my control again and begin walking hitters. I was pleased that I pitched well except for that one line drive their cleanup hitter sent over the right field fence. It was a good pitch and had plenty of movement on it, but his timing was perfect and he drilled it over the fence. Luckily we were ahead by four runs at the time.

The strength of our starting rotation was shown right from the get go. Jack had great control and several good pitches he could use, Nate was a south paw and his pitches were tough to read and he had a killer move to first base, Veldon really had a knack in getting ground ball outs and I had multiple pop flies and long outs to the outfield. We complemented each other very well.

Our schedule included games with Orem, Utah, Rick's, and Twin Falls. There were other teams we played but our toughest competition was that 'Fearsome Foursome'. I had my turn pitching to each team. Most of these games were close well-played ball games. All these teams were pretty evenly matched. And each had their stand out players. BYU has always been known for their offense. Arizona and California sent their best to play at the "Y".

Our league used the designated hitter rule during the season. A 'DH' is inserted into the lineup in place of the pitcher to increase each teams offensive output. So as a pitcher I didn't get to bat or even take hitting practice. Even bunting was left to another player. So I learned defense from my coaches. We practiced on covering first base with the ball being played by the first baseman. We were taught about backing up each and every play. No matter where the ball was hit, the pitcher has a place to go to help the defense. We even practiced some secret pickoff moves complete with signs and everything.

But each pitcher was put on the mound to do one thing. Throw strikes and keep the ball in the park. The best place to throw to almost every hitter is low in the strike zone and usually on the outside corner of the plate. I did learn from experience that there were several hitters who were low ball hitters. They loved the pitch down low and out over the plate. One of those hitters I faced played for Twin Falls.

On the Saturday that we were scheduled to travel to Twin Falls the weather decided to turn cold and the wind was blowing. Our pitching coach came up to me and handed me the game ball. "Here Barrus, you are used to pitching in this kind of weather," was all he said. He knew I was from Wyoming and he had claimed the coldest game he ever played in was in Laramie against the Wyoming Cowboys. So I was given the nod as our starting pitcher.

I quickly took my windbreaker jacket and put it under my game jersey for the entire game. I had learned that using this simple trick could save a great deal of body temperature. The temperature at game time was hovering in the high thirties and snow clouds were hanging low over the stadium. We had traveled four hours to play and didn't want to spoil the trip.

On my first trip through their batting order, I walked their third hitter after the first two had struck out. I was afraid they were going to try and send this runner down to second base on a steal. That would give their number four hitter a chance to drive him in with just a single. The runner was studying my stretch for the first pitch trying to determine when he could make his move. As I started my motion to enter my stretch, I took a quick stutter step while I spun and fired a strike to our first baseman. Their base runner didn't even move. I had completely fooled him and a tag was placed on his back by our first baseman with the ball in his glove without the base runner ever trying to get back to the base! He was out!

The game proceeded inning by inning until we batted in the top of the ninth inning. We managed to pick up a run through teamwork and a little trickery. Never the less we had a one run lead going into the bottom of the ninth. All we needed was three outs and the game was ours. Our coach came up to me before I headed to the mound and asked me," How's your arm holding up?" I told him I felt fine but I knew he was thinking of sending in a relief pitcher. He sent me to the mound but on a short leash. If any runners got on base, I would be pulled for Nate to come in and finish the game.

I was pleased with how I had pitched so far and wanted the complete game like all starting pitchers do. I also realized that I would be facing their third, fourth, and fifth hitters in the line up. They were their best hitters and I was feeling thepressure as well as the strain on my arm after pitching the entire game so far. Their third hitter had a score to settle with me since I had nailed him at first way back in the first Inning. I worked the count to two balls and two strikes when I decided another fast ball low and away just might get him. The pitch was right where I wanted it but he was looking for it in that exact spot. He jumped on it making solid contact and sending the ball whistling down the third base line. It was still gaining height when it left the park. The only thing that saved me was the Hook he gave the ball as he jumped all over that pitch. It hooked FOUL by ten feet or so. WOW! that was a close call!

But I knew I had him now. In his mind, he was out thinking the next pitch. He was thinking that I didn't want another pitch close to that last one and would be looking for a curveball inside and tight. But over the years, I almost always entered a 'K' in the strikeout column when I found myself in this same situation. I shook off the sign from my catcher a couple of times. And then I placed another fastball exactly where he had tagged that long foul ball. He was completely fooled and was only able to give it a half-hearted swing. He went down swinging! The next two hitters both grounded out to end the game. I had a 1-0 shut out!

Our JV Team went on to win the division with a solid twelve and two record. We all had made contributions to the team and felt pretty darn good about our chances to make the Varsity Team the following year. But I ended up breaking my right hand that summer which put the kybosh to that idea.

CHAPTER ELEVEN

Back to Husky Oil and Softball

Take It with A Grin of Salt

Yogi Berra

The next summer I returned to Cody to earn monies for school and a family. Jeanette and I were married that June. There were many who never thought they would ever see the day I would get married. Never the less, we were married in the Idaho Falls Temple. We returned to Cody to work. Husky Oil Company had a summer job for me and Jeanette picked up a small job at the local Gibson's department store. And I put together another softball team.

The league changed a few of the rules from the previous year. The sixteen-inch softball was scrapped for a twelve-inch 'Limited Flight' softball. And several rules that had caused heated arguments during the previous season went the way of the trash heap. But the biggest change was to our Husky Oil lineup. Most of the same players were back but this year we signed up Mr. Husky Oil himself, my dad, Tunney!

"Tunney" knew practically everybody on all the teams. He had either coached or umpired while these softballers were growing up. He was very well liked by one and all in baseball circles. Every team joined in having fun with him especially when I asked him to pitch. He would kid around with each and every hitter when they came to the plate. That was part of my strategy in using "Tunney" on the mound. I wanted to distract each hitter just enough so his timing would suffer. "Tunney" never totally grasped the concept of placing the pitch in the strike zone but out of each hitters power zone. "Tunney" viewed each pitcher as a deli-waiter serving up steaks. All he was doing was serving up a big fat softball for each hitter to clobber.

He refused to pitch after our first game, where we were beat rather soundly. He felt he could be more useful playing third base where there was more "action". This worked well to start with. Bill came in to pitch and "Tunney" was moved over to third. Jim our regular third baseman had a pretty good arm, so he was moved out to center field. Most of our hitters had learned to place hit. By timing the pitch just right, they could lob their hit just over the heads of the infielders and before the outfielders could get to it. They could also see a hole in the defense and place a ground ball in between the other players.

"Tunney" was a Pull Hitter in baseball and he was determined to continue that tradition. He would wait for an inside pitch and promptly pull it down the third base line. He was a good hitter but the other teams quickly learned where to play him. His batting average started out quite high but began to tail off as the teams got to know his hitting tendencies. "Tunney" was great fun to play with. He continually kidded around with each and every player he was close to, whether up to bat or playing defense.

Husky Oil began winning games. And team after team joined the defeated ranks by using this line up. But all good things usually come to and end. Our winning streak came to an end against Steck's IGA. But the winning streak didn't end the way most streaks usually end. They did beat us but it was the manner in how the game ended that was disturbing.

Steck's IGA had a big catcher that had just moved to town and he could really hit the ball. Late in the game he came to bat with the winning run on second base. This guy tagged a dandy up against the fence in right field. Our player fielded it cleanly but instead of throwing to home to cut down the lead runner, he threw to third base. "Tunney" was ready but the big catcher violated one of the

League's paramount rules. When a runner is involved in a close play, he is required to slide into the base. This guy probably outweighed "Tunney" by at least a hundred pounds. There was a terrible collision at third. The big catcher was called out for not sliding. But as the players cleared the base at third, there lay "Tunney" with a bone sticking out of his ankle. He was in terrible pain and the EMT's were called in. Our third baseman was out for the season with a broken ankle! Everybody was very upset especially "Tunney". Later on that night I helped him home from the hospital…Crutches and all.

CHAPTER TWELVE

BYU and a Degree in Construction Management

If the world were perfect, it wouldn't be.

Yogi Berra

Upon returning to school, we took a job in Mapleton. We lived at a Boy's Home for Juvenile Delinquents run by the State of Utah. It helped pay the bills but was hard on both Jeanette and myself. She was expecting our second child and I didn't get to play ball. No slow pitch, no baseball, no fast pitch, I was having withdrawal symptoms. But we were committed to finishing at BYU. I was working on a Composite Degree. It was actually two degrees in two related majors. The first was Industrial Education and I combined Construction Technology with that to meet the composite requirements. After our commitment in Mapleton was satisfied, we relocated back into Provo. Jeanette was busy with our two kids and I was a Teaching Assistant for one of my professors on campus.

The nice part about living in Provo again was being part of a local ward. We enjoyed somewhat regular hours and could spend more time together as a family. And during the summer months I began playing slow pitch softball again with the Elder's Quorum. I also picked up some construction work, building houses during those hot summer days.

The bunch of guys we had playing softball really meshed as friends and as a team. It wasn't long until our team had joined a City

League. We were playing a higher class of competition and we were still dominating the league. Our captain had a good grasp of the rules and our abilities. Our team had several guys who consistently hit home runs. But the league rules only allowed three home runs per inning. As soon as a fourth home run was hit the inning was over. So our captain arranged his line up with every fourth hitter being his sluggers. The idea was to get two or three runners on base and then have one of his sluggers hit a home run to clear the bases. We were consistently putting up nine or ten runs every inning with this strategy.

Our defense played well together. Teamwork was very evident when we were in the field. Our pitcher had mastered the technique of giving the hitter a strike but keeping it just far enough away from them to get a lot of ground balls. With our infield, a ground ball usually resulted in an out. I was moved from the outfield to third base when they saw how well I handled the shots hit towards third. I have quick feet and usually had the ball in glove before it crossed the baseline between third and second. Our shortstop liked to play deep, almost to the outfield. He always told me that 'anything I could get to with my glove was fair game.' He was encouraging me to field everything I could because I still had a pretty good arm and the angle I had while ranging to my left, gave me all the momentum I needed to easily throw most runners out.

Many nights we had to really juggle our transportation and players to the max. We would end up playing back-to-back games in two different leagues. If the fields were close to each other, there wasn't any problem. But if a game went into extra innings or was located across town then we would be in a bind.

One such night really stood out in my mind's eye. We finished our first game a little later than expected. We then had trouble locating the field for our next game not having played there before. We were the visiting team which meant we would hit first. I was our leadoff batter. The umpire was ready to call the game a 'NO-SHOW' when we arrived. I grabbed my bat and tossed my glove towards our dugout and scurried to the plate. It was my job to get on base, which I did. I was standing on first base and glanced at the stands where the softball fans usually sit. There was my entire team sitting in the stands. I didn't think too much about it until I headed over to the dugout at the end of our turn at bat. My glove that I had tossed in front of the dugout was gone!

Now what was I suppose to play third with, my bare hands? Everybody helped with a quick search of the area. Sure enough my hundred and fifty dollar glove was nowhere to be found! We quickly found a spare glove that was loaned to me for the night and I finished the game at third. That game ended somewhere around 11 P.M. We ended up losing, so our next tournament game was at 8 A.M. the next morning. What was I going to do for a glove tomorrow?

I got up early the next day. I still didn't have a plan for finding another loaner glove. For whatever reason I opened the front door of our apartment to look at something outside and there I saw it. A brand, spanking, new Rawlins softball glove was sitting on our porch. It had a note attached stating something about enjoying the game. I had no idea who had left this new hundred and seventy-five-dollar glove, since nobody had signed the note. I had a pretty good idea that my team was behind it but I couldn't get any of them to "FESS UP." Now I had to step up my game to justify their faith in me and the ten bucks each had thrown into the pot.

CHAPTER THIRTEEN

Graduation and Heart Mountain

We made too many wrong mistakes.

Yogi Berra

Upon graduating from BYU with a Construction Management Degree, we were led back to Wyoming. Eventually I worked on the new Husky Oil Corporate Headquarters. It was built where the old Cody Stampede grounds had stood for years. I worked doing all sorts of things. I started out as a laborer, then carpenter, and finally as an Assistant Superintendent. And of course I had to play more softball.

I played again for Husky Oil but just as a player. Not as a Coach or Manager or Scout, but just as a want-to-be star athlete. Most of the old players had gone their respective directions and my Dad was not interested in the least. I tried my hand at numerous positions. I played infield and outfield, pitcher and catcher, and even sat on the bench at times. The game is played differently depending on where a person plays. I probably learned the most while playing in the outfield.

Outfielders spend a lot of their time backing up throws and plays to each base. Nobody really notices them until they fail to back up a play. They need to back each other up constantly. Each outfielder needs a strong arm to hold each runner to as few bases as possible. They communicate with each other giving directions on where the throw needs to go and where that outfield fence is located.

I can remember one certain play when I was in center field. The ball was well hit and I was having trouble picking out the ball since it had been hit so high in the air. I have always had trouble playing under the lights anyways. The fields we play on do NOT have warning tracks next to the outfield fences. On this particular play I could have sure used one in order to have some feel for where that fence actually was.

I was completely at the mercy of my fellow fielders to let me know how I was doing. I had a bead on that ball and refused to take my eyes off of it for an instant. Just as the ball was about in my glove, I plowed directly into the chain link fence that surrounded the outfield grass. Both the ball and I went over the fence! The ball landed well out of reach for a home run and I landed on my head outside the playing field! Several players came running to see if I was hurt. Physically I was fine but my pride had been deflated for not playing the fence properly. I had failed to locate the fence with my throwing hand. I sure could have used some directions from my fellow outfielders!

I had to control my throws into the Infield better. The seams and size of the softball caused the ball to rise or tail away depending on my release and speed on the ball. I had sent many a relay to home all the way to the backstop because of a hurried throw to catch a runner. Just a micro-second longer would have allowed me to spin the ball in my hand and position the threads of the ball correctly for a perfect strike from center field instead of a catcher scrambling back at the backstop in an attempt to stop more runners from scoring. I even began gripping the ball with three fingers instead of two like I had done while playing hard ball.

As a hitter I had learned how to place the ball just about anywhere I wanted it to go. That even included hitting for a round tripper. With a little patience, and trying to hit the ball on the same trajectory it was following as it entered the strike zone, I had numerous home runs during that season. But for me, there was a lot more action and excitement created in hitting line drives through the infield. The challenge came in taking a solid single and trying to stretch it into a double.

I can remember placing a well hit drive into the right field corner. Their player had been playing out of position and I had my sights set on a triple instead of a sure double. I beat the throw into third and as the ball came to their third baseman, he couldn't handle it. The ball bounced off his leg towards left field. If I had been watching the base coach like I had been taught from every coach I had played under I would have seen him signaling me to stay on the bag. But in the excitement of the moment, I jumped up and headed for home plate.

I wasn't even half way there when the catcher caught the throw from their left fielder. I put on the brakes and turned back towards third base. Bang, I was in a hot box between third and home. I was pretty winded from my sprint around the bases and I was tagged out after just two back and forth attempts to confuse the fielders. Why hadn't I looked at the third base coach? I had committed a mental error that I knew better than attempt. Maybe next time, I would perform as I had been coached!

CHAPTER FOURTEEN

How about some Fast Pitch Softball?

You wouldn't have won, if we had beaten you.

Yogi Berra

After finishing my projects with the Nielsens, I accepted a job assignment in Riverton. I was hired to manage a concrete delivery company, Pat O'Hara Ready Mix. I hadn't been in Riverton for a year when I was invited to play fast pitch softball. The game of softball had evolved in Riverton from slow to fast pitch. What a difference! I was taken back to younger years when my Dad played on various teams around the state. There was the challenge to learn another sport and apply the skills I had acquired to fast pitch softball.

But playing was not in my immediate future. I was asked to manage a local team. Specifically, I was selected because I did not personally know any of the players. They had tried player/managers before and always ended up choosing sides. Yes, politics is a part of every sporting event on earth. Softball is no exception! The Exxon team I was asked to manage was comprised of engineers, salesman, and oil field workers from the Riverton area. I needed to manage the players based solely on their abilities.

It was easy to pick out the players that had good arms and those speedsters in the group. Offensively, it took a little longer to see who could hit and who could bunt both for a hit and for a sacrifice to move runners around the bases. When I began changing the line up, there was a gluttony of complaints. The players had obviously played with each other before and had established the order they wanted to hit in.

A team meeting was called shortly thereafter. I wanted their input into what they expected and I also wanted a chance to explain my reasons for making the changes I had made. It became evident without much ado that the players wanted to play a very upscale fast tempo style of softball. I was gratified because that was my style of game as well. Force the defense into making mistakes. We needed to get runners on base and then manipulate the game to score as many runs as possible.

I also introduced my offensive signals (signs) that I would be using as I manned the third base coach's box. I implemented the signs I had been taught while playing at BYU. 'Skin to Skin---STEAL, Skin to Blue----BUNT, and Skin to Yellow----SWING AWAY'. Each of these signs had to have an indicator in place to engage the 'SIGN'. Our indicator was the bill of my cap. I tried to keep it simple but able to conceal our intent to the opposing team's eyes. It would take a few games until everybody became accustomed to my 'SIGNS'.

The transmission of each sign was left to my trickery. I explained to them that 'Skin to Skin' was any time either one of my hands touched another part of my body with exposed skin. That could be my face or my other hand or my ears etc. But in order for the sign to be activated, I had to touch the bill of my cap first. The uniforms we wore had several different color combinations. But Blue and Yellow were the primary colors used. Our caps were Blue with Yellow lettering. The confusion usually involved me progressing through the Signs too fast and not giving the batter time to observe properly. I also cautioned each batter to allow me to continue with more signs following the transmission of the indicated sign. This helps me to keep the signals somewhat secret to opposing eyes trying to pick up on our signals. I enjoyed giving these signs and making sure our players understood them.

The next couple of games is when things began to come together. The changes I made in the line up made a real difference. The team managed to get more runners on base and then the key hitters delivered with those runners in scoring position. We were a force to be reckoned with. We were winning games left and right and many by ten runs or more. Our pitchers were commanding attention with their diversities in motions and pitch selection.

About half way through the season, an All-Star game was scheduled with a team from Powell coming to town. I was chosen as the Manager to represent Riverton. I was dumbfounded. On the one side I was eager to try what I had learned about the game, and then on the other side I wondered if we would be playing against a bunch of ball players that I knew in high school. We practiced just once before the big game. I had some good players to work into the lineup. Like most All-Star teams that are put together, I had fifteen players that all wanted to play. The big question was who to start and who to sit.

In the early minutes of the game, both teams were struggling against superior pitching. But on the second cycle through our batting order, things began to click. We were able to get two players on base. This was courtesy of a throwing error by their third baseman. And then one of the players from Exxon connected on a monster home run. We had the lead and I was determined to keep it. By aggressive base running and a stingy defense, we increased our lead to five runs with two innings to go.

Powell made a run at us. They connected on back-to-back doubles, which swung the momentum in their favor. A dropped line drive by our right fielder produced another run. We had a two run advantage with their top hitters coming to bat. As a manager I did not have any players left on the bench that I knew could pitch. So I used a little management trickery. I had our first baseman and pitcher trade places. The change in velocity and motion had their hitters back on their heels. I used this pitcher to finish the inning and then I brought back the first pitcher from first and moved our pitcher back to first. The simple strategy worked. We won the game and I gained a lot of respect from the players because of my knowledge of the rules. I had a little fun with the guy who hit the home run by insisting that the home run sign I had given him was the difference in the ball game. Fast pitch softball can be a lot of fun!

That season ended in success with Exxon winning the City Championship. But the following year, a rocky road presented itself. The popularity of the sport was increasing with two additional teams entering the division. Those additional teams had pulled several players from the Exxon team to play for them. We found ourselves barely making a full roster by the start of league play. The members of the team approached me with another novel idea. They knew I could play and proposed I function as a Player/Coach. When enough players showed up for a game, I would continue to coach and manage like last year. But when we came up short players, I would be entered as a player.

Things began well enough. The first few games were played with enough players to man the field. But the employees of Exxon can be transferred on the drop of a hat. We lost our right fielder who was sent to Evanston. So I found myself playing right field or catcher for every game.

A coach always plays the outfielder with the best arm in right field. But a lot of teams seem to play their weakest defensive player in that position. I had to earn the respect of the opposing teams. It didn't take long to encounter a situation that would challenge my abilities.

In my first game as our right fielder, we found ourselves facing their fastest base runner early in the game. He promptly doubled down the leftfield line. The hitter directly behind him in the order hit a clean single to my side of the outfield. I fielded the well-hit ball cleanly. I could hear my fellow fielders yelling" He's trying to score!" I fired the ball to the plate on a line drive. It arrived home a good two steps ahead of the runner. But what should have been an easy out with our catcher applying the tag instead resulted in an error by our catcher. When he did apply the tag he was only using his glove hand, the ball was knocked free and the run scored. But everybody there saw that I was quick and accurate with my throw. I was not that easy to score on as many had been thinking.

We did go on to win that ball game and many subsequent games as well. But just as I was feeling comfortable as an outfielder, our catcher was transferred out of the area. I rearranged the defense, which found me catching behind the plate. I was able to use my past experience as a pitcher to our advantage on the receiving end of our rotation.

Rick was a seasoned pitcher and player. He was doubtful I could handle the position. But following that first game, I had earned his respect as well. I was not afraid to challenge the runners either by gunning them down when stealing or by blocking the plate on a close play at home. However, I cost Rick his shutout with a close play at home.

The opposing team had a runner on third and Rick delivered a low curve that hit the front lip of the plate and bounced past me. I spun around, located the ball, and reached out to the plate with the ball in my glove. I was diving to beat the runner to the plate. Instead of a sweeping tag like I usually apply, I just laid the ball and glove in front of the plate to let the runner slide into it. I must have been too early as the runner saw his opportunity and slid to the far side of the plate. Safe! Yelled the ump. I argued with his call as did Rick but never the less the call stood. My saving grace was that our offense out scored them for the win.

That season was going to be my last as a player. My son was joining a Tee Ball League next year, and I was planning on coaching him and his friends. So when given the chance to play in the area championship, I agreed. We had a pretty good bunch of athletes. They all played well together and respected each other's abilities and standards. Our first tournament was scheduled in Powell.

I don't understand how I always get to play the tournament favorites for our first game. But here we go again. Powell vs Riverton was scheduled as game number one on day one of the invitational. We had heard a lot about the program in Powell. It had been in existence much longer than the one in Riverton. Over the years they had developed some splendid teams and some very fine pitchers. The one we were scheduled to see in our first game was a veteran from years of participation and hours of practice.

Vern Ackerman was ten years our elder. But don't let that fool anybody; he could still bring it with the best of them. He had developed a 'Riser' that was rumored to be unhittable. I have heard that in many circles both in baseball and in softball. Just let me say 'Seeing is Believing'. We were confident in our offensive and defensive capabilities. It promised to be a good game.

The game was scheduled to begin at six o'clock just as most of the town would be getting off work. Powell would definitely have the home field advantage. And being the visiting team would put us hitting first. We had the opportunity to score right out of the shoot. Davey would be hitting first and I would be right behind him. He had a real knack in getting on base and I would move him into scoring position for our hard-hitting three, four, &five hitters.

Davey did not disappoint. He slapped the first pitch right back at their pitcher. He was fast and beat the throw to first. My job was to get him to second base at all costs. I prided myself in being a good to excellent bunter. So on his first pitch, I squared to sacrifice bunt Davey over to second base. And that is when I witnessed his 'Riser' first hand. As the ball came into the strike zone, I extended my bat to meet the ball.

At the last second, the ball 'hopped' in its trajectory. It was just enough to cause a foul ball instead of a perfect bunt down the first base line.

I had been taken by surprise. But now that I had seen his pitch I was certain I could handle it again. On the next pitch I slid my hands further up on the bat to give me better bat control and squared to bunt again. Same pitch and the same result! I was sure they wouldn't expect another bunt attempt with two strikes against me. A fouled bunt on the third strike is the same as a strike out. I heard my dugout hollering to me to 'bunt the top of the ball' so on the next pitch I committed early and squared for another bunt. I was certain I could put down that bunt. But the 'Riser' got the best of me. I fouled off that pitch as well and heard the umpire bark "Three strikes you're out"!

The rest of the game proceeded in a very similar pattern. Anytime we put a runner on base, we were unable to move him up and score. Vern Ackerman had pitched a shut out to open the tournament. And we were the victims. We never recovered from that first game. We ended up losing our next game as well and were out of the tournament all together.

CHAPTER FIFTEEN

Coaching My Children

*I tell the kids, somebody's gotta win, somebody's
gotta lose. Just don't fight about it.
Just try to get better.*

Yogi Berra

There is quite a difference between semi-pro ball and first year tee ball. I had to make the transition. I had coached legion ball, Babe Ruth ball, and City League softball but Tee Ball was going to be a real challenge for me. I had spent time with my children playing catch and batting the ball around. They were just getting the basics down. The glove is used to catch the ball when it is thrown to. The right hand is above the left hand when batting. And when throwing the ball with your right hand, you always take a step with your left foot first. But having a dozen kids who do not have these basics down was definitely going to be interesting.

I had an assistant coach, Harvey, who hadn't played that much himself but really enjoyed kids. Besides he had three boys on the team. I can remember looking into the mirror after our first practice and asking myself, "What have I gotten myself into?" But if the other Dads could do it then I could too.

Our next practice was devoted to 'catching the ball'! I can still hear myself instructing them to "Always Use Two Hands" Those baseball gloves are huge for those beginning players. And far too many of them have watched their older brothers or fathers catch the ball repeatedly with just one hand. They just don't realize that their hand muscles are not developed enough to squeeze that ball with enough pressure to keep it in the glove. It always seems to find a way out of the glove and down to the ground. Besides if your "throwing hand" is close to the ball after you catch it, then it is much quicker and easier to grab the ball and then throw it again. Another point that needs to be made is 'Wait for the ball to hit the glove before putting your other hand in the glove" It can really hurt when the ball strikes your bare knuckles first instead of the glove.

We had a real struggle in teaching them how to hold the glove depending on where the ball has been thrown. If the ball is thrown below your waist the glove needs to be placed to resemble a bowl. It is just easier that way. And if the ball is thrown above your waist them turn the glove completely over so the palm of the glove is facing the ball. It is very awkward to reverse the position of the glove. Oh, I almost forgot the "Cool" part of using the glove. On television the pros always seem to be wearing a batting glove inside the baseball glove. I don't know how it all started but a player isn't 'Cool' unless he has a skin-tight golfing glove on under his ball glove.

All of the players show up to practice wanting to bat. Many even have their own bats that they have purchased brand spanking new. Our next lesson was on 'how do we hold the bat?" The law of probability would dictate that at least half of the team would get the correct hand above the other one when holding the bat correctly. I was to find out otherwise. They were determined to place their left hand on top of their right hand when batting right handed. They really do not understand which hand does the hitting (it is always the lower hand). A right-handed hitter uses his right hand to just guide the bat. The power comes from a batter's left hand, the opposite hand. So we practiced our swing fifty times before we ever placed a ball on the tee.

I noticed right away that most of the players were watching where the ball was suppose to go rather than concentrating on the ball itself. "Keep your eye on the ball!' was my war cry. Coordination can only come through repetition. So we began swinging with a ball perched on that rubber tee. The number of swings that actually strike the ball instead of the tee itself goes down the more a batter practices his swing.

I had to correct several players that were swinging "up" at the ball. A nice level swing will produce "line drives" which is what I was after. A hard hit line drive will result in more hits than a 'fly ball' every time.

I had a few unusual situations on our team that first year. Both my son and my oldest daughter were on the team. It took a while but the boys had to accept the fact that a 'girl' can play just as good as a 'boy' and many times better. And I had a couple of left-handed players on the team as well. All the instructions had to be repeated in 'Southpaw' terms so they could compete.

As we were getting ready to begin league play, I helped the team set some goals. We may not win any games but we would always encourage our fellow players in their efforts. Nothing can kill team spirit quicker than finding fault with fellow teammates. Each player will get a hit this season and each player will assist in getting an out when in the field at sometime during the season. Other than that, we just wanted to have some fun.

Our first game was upon us. I wanted our best player on first base. He needed to catch every ball that was thrown to him. Our fastest players were placed in the outfield to chase down any fly balls or overthrows they could. The players that could throw with some sense of accuracy were placed on the left side of the infield and our biggest player would be our catcher. Not because of any pending collisions but just so the catching equipment would fit him better. So with a few substitutes, we began our first game of the season.

We were scheduled to bat first. I let my assistant handle the batting order. He chose to just let them hit according to the position that they were playing. Number one is the pitcher; Number two is the catcher and so on down the line. Strategy would have to come later as each player developed and we as the coaches learned what each player was able to do. About all I remember from that first inning was the ball being thrown haphazardly around the bases in an attempt to get a player out. I guess the best adjective I could use is 'Organized Chaos'. The players learned quickly to just get the ball back to the pitcher. A rule was in place that nobody could advance to another base as long as the pitcher had the ball and was standing inside the pitching circle.

But there wasn't any lack for action as the players from both teams proceeded to 'Clobber' that ball from on top of the tee.

I can remember watching my children play. The oldest daughter, Danny Lyn, preceded to take charge of the players closest to her by making sure they were in position. She had seen her cousins and Dad play in dozens of games and had a pretty good idea where everybody was supposed to be. I also noticed that my son, Jesse, had a 'inside-out' swing. He was always hitting the ball to the right side of the field. That isn't good or bad but just the way things are.

I can also remember hearing some very negative comments from one member of our team towards the other team. I nipped that off in the bud. We were not going to find fault with a member of either team. I didn't care if they were doing it to us or not. I was pleased that the players on our team corrected themselves early. I don't remember the score of that game but felt pretty good about our team's performance and excitement for the game.

Our team did win most of the games that year. But more importantly the team goals that had been set early were being reached. Each player had learned to hit the ball well. They had learned to rely on each other as members of a team and not just a bunch of individual players trying to win ball games. But our center fielder had yet to make a defensive play by himself. He had made numerous attempts but always seemed to come up short. He either dropped the fly ball or made an arrant throw to another player letting additional runs score. He was convinced that he wasn't good enough.

It had come down to the last game of the year. Each team was scoring runs and each had a chance to win the game. But our center fielder would be the difference. In the last inning, the other team had one last chance to score and decide the game. With two outs, their player delivered a long fly ball towards right centerfield. The race was on. The ball was sinking fast but just as it was about to hit the ground our centerfielder sticks out his glove. He has the ball wedged tightly in the web of his glove! The catch was made and our team did in fact win the game! The following day we had scheduled a large barbeque for the team and their families. They were still talking about that catch our centerfielder had made to end the season

CHAPTER SIXTEEN

Little League and Politics

*You've got to be very careful if you
don't know where you are going,
because you might not get there.*

Yogi Berra

Most people that here the words Little League have mixed feelings about the experience. There are people who live and breath baseball. They just know that their son will be playing in the Major Leagues someday. And there are people who just want to see their children playing a game they enjoyed as a youngster. I probably landed somewhere in between these two extremes.

Growing up I spent practically every spare summer afternoon either at practice or playing in a game somewhere. So when my children reached the age for Little League, I tried to teach them about the game. I was divided between coaching and providing for my family. As a contractor in Wyoming, I had the summer months to glean the monies needed for the winter that would follow. Winter in Wyoming is legendary. As a parent, I could see potential in my children. And there was something in their genes that allowed them to perform well in baseball.

I tried coaching in multiple leagues and age groups. As a tee ball coach, I found out quickly how big a role a parent can play in a child's performance. The ability to hit and catch a ball are essential to the game and it became very evident which players had received help at home. As a coach I was continually under the microscope from parents about their child. Is he playing enough? Is he playing at the position the parents want him to play? Is he batting like they have seen him do at home? Why can't their child use the bat we just bought him? These and a million other issues surface. It is no wonder that good Little league coaches are hard to find.

I was also coaching against other coaches that varied in experience and technical know-how of the game. I have had opposing coaches approach me for clarification on rules and how they can help certain players improve. I have also coached against coaches that just have to win at all costs. Even if that means they bend some of the rules to accomplish that. Many times the umpires that call the games are severely lacking in their abilities. I have seen opposing coaches take advantage of this inexperience to gain advantage during a game. It is sad to see how some coaches treat their players and their opponents during each game.

I have also seen a few select coaches that are very positive and courteous to all they come in contact with. They just seem to bring out the best in each player they work with. These coaches gain the respect of each and every parent very quickly by their positive attitudes and respect shown everybody. They may or may not know the game inside and out but they learn from each practice and game. They are just fun to be around!

My son was privileged to play under one such coach. Rich was very well known in the community. And he was a boy's coach. They would give him one hundred and ten per cent during every game and practice. I worked with him as an assistant coach for the Yankees in our local Little League. I could always count on him to say or do the right thing no matter what the situation was. He did not have a family or boys on the team. But he knew each boy very well.

The Riverton Yankees were always a contending team. Rich had a keen eye for talent. But Rich also had coaches that just hated to be beat by his teams. Larry was one such coach. He knew the game well and used any scheme he could come up with to beat the Yankees. As we progressed through several seasons, the Indians and the Yankees almost always were at the top of their division. We would win some games against them and we would also lose a few. But they were always close.

The game I remember the most was when my son, Jess was twelve years old. In Little League that is the last year anyone can play. They move up to a different league when they turn thirteen. We had several twelve year olds on the Yankee team that year. Jess usually played in center field due to his speed and strong arm. Kara, another twelve-year-old, played second base for us, and Jeremy was our best pitcher. As a pitcher, it is critical to throw strikes and avoid walking the opposing hitters. Jess and Kara had both tried pitching but had trouble finding the strike zone. But all three of them could hit the ball.

As I remember the situation, it was a really close game with the Yankees trailing the Indians by single run going into the bottom of the sixth and final inning. The Indians had their star pitcher on the mound. They did manage to get two outs on us but we had also filled the bases. There we were with the bases loaded and my son coming to bat. Larry, the opposing coach, knew my son's tendency to hit to the right side of the field. So he calls time and shifts his defense to the right side. I was wondering what was going through Jess's mind at that moment.

He knew the Indian pitcher, Levi, could really bring it with his fastball. Jess had reached base a couple of times by placing the ground balls between first and second base. But now the Indians had a good fielding infielder playing directly on that spot. As I looked at my son's face I could see him set his jaw with determination written all over his face. The first two pitches were high and outside. They were pitching him trying to get him to ground another ball to the shifted defense. But on the next pitch I saw Jess turn on that pitch and connect on a screaming line drive towards deep left field!

As I was watching the flight of that line drive I can remember yelling," Get out of here, Get out of here!" Sure enough, that line drive cleared the fence by at least ten feet! Jess had hit a Grand Slam Home Run! The fans were all going crazy as each of the four base runners crossed home plate. The Yankees had spoiled the Indians perfect season by beating them during the last game of the year!

In the week following that victory, several of our team members were voted on the All-Star Team. Jess and Kara were among those chosen. Even though we had defeated the Indians on the last game of the year, they were declared the league champions having only one defeat. The Yankees had lost several games during that year. The league had a tradition that allowed the coach from the championship team to coach the All-Star Team. So Larry, the coach of the Indians, was given the reins of the Riverton All-Star Team. The assistant position was offered to Rich but he had to refuse it due to the time constraints. Practice started immediately with two-a-day practices mandatory. Larry was bound and determined to win that pending state championship and prove to everybody that he was the best coach in our league.

As the practices began, the favorite players of Coach Larry became obvious. Most of the players from the Indians were placed in the starting positions. And the players from the Yankees that had defeated him on that last day were placed on the bench. Their services may or may not be needed in the ensuing tournament. That year the State Little League Tournament was to be held in Green River. It was a four- hour trip one-way and most of the parents that wanted to support the team traveled there for the week.

I can still remember that first game of the tournament. The Riverton Little League was soundly beat by a big and talented Laramie club. And the strength of the Riverton team, hitting, did not develop at all. But several players that had made the team did not even get a chance to play. Jess and Kara were two of the players that sat on the bench the entire game. The parents were totally upset. Charlie, Kara's father, was the most vocal of the bunch. He had taken time off work like the rest of the parents and did not even get to see his daughter play at all. At the conclusion of the parent's meeting, Larry promised to start the kids who did not play in the first game into the lineup of the second and possibly their last game.

Their opponent for the second game was Rock Springs. Rock Springs is just a stone's throw from Green River so the hometown advantage was definitely in their favor. Larry was true to his promise and Kara was playing second base and batting in the lead off spot.

Jess was playing right field and hitting number two. They wasted no time in showing what they could do. They both began the game with solid hits and went on in to score. This repeated itself throughout the game. The Riverton bats had come alive with Kara and Jess leading the way.

This same leadoff pair continued to lead the way and score through the next three games. Everyone was convinced they were the key to sparking the Riverton offense except Larry. He decided to insert a couple of his favorites back into the leadoff hitters for the next game. It was as if the spark plug had been removed from the engine. The offense never got moving at all. Riverton was defeated again and handed their traveling papers back home. Riverton was in an uproar about how Larry had cost them the tournament. Larry's coaching blunders had led the team into two defeats they could have easily won by playing up to their potential. I don't know if Riverton was the best team there or not. But I did see how home town politics can destroy a team and turn a game that is to be played for fun into a nightmare for all involved.

That same coaching mentality that Larry demonstrated in All-Stars was prevalent with the Babe Ruth coaches that selected Jess to play for their squad of thirteen year olds. Jess was not having fun like he had under Rich as a coach. He decided to leave the team. Church softball was just coming of age in Fremont County and my children were some of the first in line. I elected to sit out as one of the coaches and root as a faithful parent from the sidelines. I was determined to watch the game and keep my mouth shut no matter what happened. I joined the silent majority who attended what games I could while offering advice to my children when it was asked for. That is a very hard position to be in. I was determined to not let politics get in the road of the kids having a good time.

Church softball in Riverton was just getting started. The girls and the boys were organized differently. The seasons were divided with the boy's season first followed by the girls. The softball fields that were used to play the games needed to be shared with the city leagues. But the main goal of the league was to enjoy the sport and not get so rapped up in winning/losing and tournament play. It was quite refreshing to see my children taking the lead in the sport.

One event that I vividly remember was the Father-Son Softball game. Not because of the talent displayed or the great food that appeared after the game but because of the injury I suffered during the game. My son was playing right field and this particular field did not have an outfield fence. So if a ball managed to get by any of the outfielders, it was Katie-bar-the-door. The runners would take as many bases as they could while the ball was being chased down. I was determined to send my son chasing the ball all the way to the highway if possible.

I waited on the perfect outside pitch and sent it screaming into the gap between right field and center. But I had forgotten how fast my son could cover ground. As I was rounding first at full speed, I catch a glimpse of my son as he cut the ball off before it bounded past the outfielders. I applied the brakes and then wheeled around to head back to first base. I was over half way to second base by then and would have probably been gunned down if I had continued. I knew my son had a pretty good arm and was as accurate as they come. So I slide into first base head first. The ball reached the base at the same time my head did. BOOM! I was drilled right in the ear by the ball that had been rifled in to the first baseman!

Immediately I suffered shell shock. The hearing in my ear was replaced with a unmistakable ringing and as I grabbed the side of my head, I noticed my hand had blood all over it. I could hear my base coach yelling," Run, run to second!" The ball had deflected off the side of my head into the crowd. But I wasn't going anywhere except to the emergency room at the hospital! Once there they informed me that my eardrum had been pierced and with care it would heal itself in six to eight weeks!

I was given some eardrops and specific instructions about keeping water out of that ear until it healed. Wow! Eight weeks without a shower is really going to stink up the whole house! But by listening a little closer, I learned how to keep the ear protected while showering. The ringing lasted for a few more days and the ear let me know anytime I got moisture inside. Instant pain! But I managed to get through it and don't blame anybody for the accident except myself. To this day, all my kids remember is that Dad could whistle through through his ear! Awesome!

Every time I watch my girls in sports, I can see their Scottish heritage coming to the surface. My mother can be as stubborn as they come when told she cannot do something she really wants to do. My sisters and my daughters all follow her lead. My youngest daughter wanted to be one of the first girls in the family to play Little League baseball. She was advised by several people to just stick to softball, but she signed up for tee ball in spite of their pleadings. She was drafted on to a team of all boys. They were not just any boys but most of them were in her class at school. But the die was cast and she suited up for her first game.

I think it was in the second inning. She came up to the plate to take her swings. She has always had pretty good hand to eye coordination. On her first swing she makes solid contact and the ball heads towards second base. She takes off running as fast as she can. Karen has always been fleet footed but there was one small problem. She was running towards third base instead of first! Karen was running the bases backwards! She knew better having watched dozens of games and practiced for hours but the umpire had to call her out anyways. The rest of her team never forget the miscue and were reminding her frequently which way to run after hitting the ball. How embarrassing!

EPILOGUE

I continue to be a spectator and enjoy watching my grandchildren play the game. They occasionally ask me about a rule interpretation or how could they improve a certain technique. But I try not to be too judgmental of their abilities and team efforts. I have even stepped in as an Assistant Coach to help my son and daughters coach their children. I continue to take the game to levels that most are not ready to achieve or even want to. I take the game way too seriously.

My children are great motivators when it comes to sports and coaching. They have put me on a pedestal that is far higher than I ever achieved. They are far better coaches and parents than I ever dreamed possible. I am surprised that they still ask me about the finer points of the game, even though I can't run or throw anymore. And they each enjoy a good laugh at some of the blunders we each made while playing **America's Favorite Pastime.**

www.ingramcontent.com/pod-product-compliance
Lightning Source LLC
LaVergne TN
LVHW011733060526
838200LV00051B/3163